Working with Children
of
Mixed Parentage

Edited by

Tovin Okitikpi

Russell House Publishing

First published in 2005 by:
Russell House Publishing Ltd.
4 St. George's House
Uplyme Road
Lyme Regis
Dorset DT7 3LS

Tel: 01297-443948
Fax: 01297-442722
e-mail: help@russellhouse.co.uk
www.russellhouse.co.uk

British Library Cataloguing-in-publication Data:
A catalogue record for this book is available from the British Library.

ISBN: 1-903855-64-0

Typeset by Saxon Graphics Ltd, Derby

Printed by Arrowsmith, Bristol

About Russell House Publishing

RHP is a group of social work, probation, education and youth and community work practitioners and academics working in collaboration with a professional publishing team.

Our aim is to work closely with the field to produce innovative and valuable materials to help managers, trainers, practitioners and students.

We are keen to receive feedback on publications and new ideas for future projects.

For details of our other publications please visit our website or ask us for a catalogue. Contact details are on this page.

Contents

Acknowledgements

This book was inspired through discussions with a countless number of people interested in highlighting the experiences of people of mixed parentage and in improving the lives of the children in the care system. I am grateful for the foresight and inspiration of Professor John Pitts and his tireless pursuit of social justice, equality and the genuine empowerment of others, be they academics, students, practitioners or those in receipt of services. I would like to say a special thank you to all the authors who contributed to this book and especially to Cathy Aymer for her insightfulness and challenges. Although all the contributors were very busy with their research, teaching commitments and other engagements they nevertheless made time to put down their ideas so that others may benefit from their expertise.

About the Authors

The Editor

Dr Toyin Okitikpi, FRSA is Principal Lecturer and Course Director of social work at London South Bank University, London. His PhD study explored the experiences of black men and white women in interracial relationships, how they manage their relationships and the adaptive processes that have been developed to enable them to manage their relationships. He has a wide range of experience in social work and although his practice experience has been within the specialist area of children and families, his recent writings have concentrated on social and practice issues within social work and social work education. His interests include social work education, the importance of education in the lives of children and young people, refugee and asylum-seeking children and their families, social integration and cohesion, and interracial/multi-cultural families and their experiences.

The Contributors

Dr Ravinder Barn is Senior Lecturer in Applied Social Studies in the Department of Social and Political Science, Royal Holloway, University of London. She has researched and published widely into the situation of children of mixed parentage and their families.

Annabel Goodyer is Senior Lecturer and an MA Course Director at the London South Bank University. Her PhD is on foster children as consumers of fostering services. Research interests include social work education, children and families and issues about Children's Rights. She is co-author of *The Teaching of Communication in Social Work Courses: SCIE Research Review.*

Vicki Harman is a PhD research student at Royal Holloway, University of London.

Dr Ilan Katz is Deputy Director at the Policy Research Bureau. He has had many years of policy, practice and research experience in children's services. He started his career as a social worker and manager in local authorities and the voluntary sector, and was head of practice development and research at the NSPCC. He was Team Leader of the Children's Fund policy team in the Children and Young People's Unit, and Head of the Children in Need and Family Support Section of the DfES. He has written extensively on issues of race and ethnicity and on child protection and family support. He is the author of *The Construction of Racial Identity in Children of Mixed Parentage: Mixed Metaphors* (1996) and co-edited (with Amal Treacher) *The Dynamics of Adoption* (2000). More recently he co-authored a publication on the future of child welfare for the think tank DEMOS (Cooper, Hetherington and Katz, 2003) and co-edited *Evaluating Family Support: Thinking Critically, Thinking Internationally* (Katz and Pinkerton, 2003).

Dr Gillian Olumide is a Lecturer in Social Policy at the School of Health Science at the University of Wales, Swansea. She has presented national and international papers on the experiences of children of mixed parentage and on children's health and development in general. She is co-author of a report to the Department of Health Research Project, *Patients as Partners: Children and the NHS* and the author of *Raiding the Gene Pool: the Social Construction of Mixed Race,* (2002), London, Pluto Press.

Dr Charlie Owen is Senior Research Officer at the Thomas Coram Foundation Research Unit at the Institute of Education, University of London. His main research interest is the secondary analysis of official statistics. He also teaches research methods and the use of computers for both qualitative and quantitative analysis. He is a member of the Radical Statistics Group.

Dr Kwame Owusu-Bempah is a Senior Lecturer at Leicester University.

Dr Lena Robinson is Senior Lecturer in Psychology and Social Work at the University of Birmingham and has been in social work education for many years. She is the author of: *Psychology for Social Workers: Black Perspectives* (1995); *Race, Communication and the Caring Professions* (1998); and *Cross-Cultural Child Development for Social Workers* (Macmillan, in press).

Professor June Thoburn, CBE, is Professor of Social Work at the University of East Anglia. She was the founding Director of the Centre for Research on the Child and Family at UEA. A qualified and experienced child and family social worker, she has been teaching on and researching across the field of child welfare since 1978. Professor Thoburn also has interests in international aspects of child and family social work, and has links with child welfare researchers and agencies in Hong Kong, Japan, China, Australia, New Zealand, Sweden and USA.

Dr Amal Treacher is a Lecturer at the Centre for Psychosocial Studies, Birkbeck College. She has written widely on matters of ethnicity and postcolonial subjectivity; and she is mixed race – white/English/Christian mother, and Egyptian/Muslim father. She is currently working on a book exploring everyday life in London and Cairo.

Chapter 1

Working with Children of Mixed Parentage

Toyin Okitikpi

Introduction

How children from interracial backgrounds fit into the Anglo-American racial and cultural binary world continues to generate controversy on both sides of the Atlantic. During the 1980s there were robust discussions about how such children should be classified and how social workers and social welfare professionals ought to respond to their needs. In Britain research evidence points to the high numbers of 'black' children being looked after by local authorities, however the use of the term 'black' has not been particularly helpful in differentiating between the experiences of children from African-Caribbean and southern Asian background and children of mixed parentage. The social work profession's approach towards children of mixed parentage has tended to owe more to a simplistic interpretation of the children's racial identity and their cultural affiliations rather than an informed understanding or appreciation of their interracial background and their self perceptions.

Guided by a binary world view and an essentialist ideology, on the one hand, and an unquestioning acceptance of the 'one-drop rule' on the other, the discourses concerning these children still appear to be bounded by a 16th Century racialised ideology rather than an 'enlightened' 21st century understanding of the social and personal experiences of the children.

In the face of these beliefs and attitudes, in Britain, an increasing number of publications have attempted to explore the experiences of people of mixed heritage. Parker and Song (2001) analyse the ideas that underpin mixed race categorisations, revealing the contradictory logic within the discourse, an area explored in detail in this volume by Charlie Owen. Small (1986), Banks (1992, 1995), Maxime (1993) and Prevatt-Goldstein (1999) address social work with children of mixed parentage, but from a premise that tends to pathologise the children and their families and fails to take account of the totality of the children's background. Phoenix and Tizard (1993), Alibhai-Brown (2001) and Katz (1996) do address the experiences of children of mixed parentage and, in their different ways, contribute to the debate about identity, but none explore, in any detail, how welfare professionals might best work with such children.

The present volume differs significantly from some previous work, being built upon two important pillars; namely that children of mixed parentage should not simply be defined as 'black' and that it is possible for the children to develop a positive, integrated, sense of self that draws upon and celebrates their dual heritage.

For this reason, this volume attempts to give a reasoned critique of the binary worldview and highlights its impact upon policy and practice vis-a-vis mixed race families. One of the aims is to offer an account of the lived experience of mixed race families rooted in empirical research and to identify the particular problems faced by mixed race families and their children and their socio-cultural needs. Ultimately the aim is to indicate the ways in which agency policies, which take account of these problems and needs, might be developed and to identify the implications for effective intervention by welfare professionals.

Mixed Responses

In order to fully appreciate the experiences of children of mixed parentage it is important to take account of their family background and to consider the extent to which the attitudes held about the children's parents' relationship (the interracial partnership) affects the ways the children are perceived and dealt with by social workers and other welfare professionals. Prevatt-Goldstein (1999) for example, often refers to mixed race children as 'black children with a white mother,' similarly Banks (1995) and Maxime (1993) have no difficulty referring to the children of mixed parentage as 'black'. In so doing, they suggest that the children are by-products of a relationship that is, at best, difficult to understand and essentially unacceptable. They pose an implicit critique of interracial relationships per se and in doing so echo many other contributors to this field who still appear to find it difficult to understand why anyone would want to form an intimate relationship with a person from a different ethnicity and cultural background (Alibhai-Brown and Montague, 1992). Indeed Katz (1996) raises precisely this question when he asks: 'Why do people from different racial groups form liaisons which produce children of mixed parentage, given the antagonism between races? What are the interpersonal dynamics in such liaisons?' (Katz, 1996: 24) Indeed, although interracial relationships have been an area of both interest and concern, both scholarly and popular, since black and white people first encountered each other (Fryer, 1985; Henriques, 1974; Alibhai-Brown and Montague, 1992).

Interestingly, Alibhai-Brown and Montague (1992) discovered that:

> *Before colonisation and slavery there was no evidence of any deep feelings of distaste and prejudice towards certain physical characteristics. Academics who have studied the history of miscegenation – in the West, in the ancient world and during early Christianity – have found that although there was awareness of colour and physical difference, dark skin was seen as sensuous and attractive. Ovid described his love for a black slave girl in Amores and Herodotus thought that*

the Ethiopians were 'the tallest and handsomest men in the world'. It is well known that Moses loved Tharbis, also an Ethiopian, and liaisons between the Egyptians and the Romans all reveal an absence of the barriers which came later.
(Alibhai-Brown and Montague, 1992: 5)

An illogical partnership

Although Alibhai-Brown and Montague are highlighting the fact that sexual interest between black and white people has a long history, the subtext of Katz's (1996) questioning is that interracial relationships, in certain socio-cultural contexts are illogical. Why, he asks, would anyone want to form an intimate relationship with someone from a different cultural background if the relationship is subject to disapprobation and is likely to provoke hostility from both black and white significant others and strangers. Katz's questioning should not be interpreted negatively, since his aim is not to denigrate such relationships. On the contrary it is an important question because it encourages a deeper examination of the context in which the interracial relationship takes place and, by extension, of the very nature of the relationship between black and white people in that context. But Katz is also asking us to consider the profound social ambivalence to interracial relationships and the kind of social world they portend in a socially fragmented, multiracial, environment.

For both black and white observers the interracial relationship may symbolise a breakdown of that which was previously held to be 'normal'; challenging naturalistic assumptions, about appropriate social, cultural and sexual boundaries. The interracial relationship threatens the clearly demarcated binary world rendering prior notions of racial and cultural purity unsustainable.

Making sense of interracial relationships

Whereas the motivation of those entering same-race relationships tends to be regarded as fairly unproblematic, there is a fairly widespread view that interracial relationships do not *just* happen by accident. There is often a perception that those involved, particularly the black partners, are motivated by the desire for social status, self-betterment or worse. It is possible to identify at least seven popular accounts of what it is that motivates people to enter interracial relationships. The accounts are:

1. Racial denial and self-hatred, particularly by the black partner.
2. The quest for cultural inclusion and social mobility.
3. The quest for economic mobility.
4. Sexual and colour curiosity.
5. Revenge for racial and social oppression.
6. Geographical propinquity and shortage of same race partners.
7. Mutual affection and shared interests.

1. Racial denial and self-hatred. Shahrazad Ali (1989) has argued that the black partner's embrace (both metaphorical and actual) of a white partner represent a denial of their own blackness. This view owes much to the writings of Franz Fanon and, in particular, to the idea that the psychological process of the black partner in the relationship is powered by the desire to become *white* and that this can only be realised through forming a relationship with a white partner. This is a view that has a long history. For example, Louis-T Achille, in his report to the interracial conference in Paris in 1949 asserted that:

> *Insofar as truly interracial marriage is concerned, one can legitimately wonder to what extent it may not represent for the coloured spouse a kind of subjective consecration to wiping out himself and in his own mind the colour prejudice from which he has suffered so long...*

> (Louis-T Achille, 1949, in Fanon, F. 1952: 9)

He continues:

> *Some men or some women, in effect, by choosing partners of another race, marry persons of a class or a culture inferior to their own whom they would not have chosen as spouses in their own race and whose chief asset seems to be assurance that the partner will achieve denaturalisation and 'de-racialisation'.*

> (ibid)

2. The quest for cultural inclusion and social mobility. Wade (1993) and Warren and Johnson (1994) argue that a black person seeking inclusion in the socio-cultural mainstream in predominantly white societies may express that desire through a willingness to identify with, and conform to the dominant values of society. The assumption is that in a society in which there is an implicit 'ranking' of racial groups within it those who want to belong and be part of the dominant group can get there by forming a relationship with, in the British case, a white partner.

3. The quest for economic mobility. Ferguson (1982), highlighted the, often argued, point that a black person seeking individual economic advancement in a predominantly white society may attempt to achieve this by acquiring a white partner. This account is based upon the demonstrable reality of the poor economic circumstances of a majority of black families in the UK and racial discrimination in the job market (Modood et al., 1997; Jones et al., 1998). This argument holds that certain black people, particularly black men, believe that if they adopt the trappings of 'whiteness', an interracial partnership being key amongst them, and minimise their 'black' affiliations, they will be better able to penetrate the white economic world and, as a result, gain access to enhanced career and business opportunities.

4. Sexual and colour curiosity. This explanation suggests that sexual and colour curiosity, with its attendant fantasies about 'black' and 'white' sexuality, is the key motivating factor in the formation of interracial relationships. This belief is articulated most clearly in Bastide's (1961) essay *Dusky Venus and Black Apollo* and forms the central motif in Spike Lee's film Jungle Fever. These sexualisations of colour, in which fanciful, exotic sexual characteristics and possibilities are attributed to the other race partner, are deemed to be operating at both the conscious and unconscious levels. The thrill of transgressing social and cultural taboos and legal prohibitions in societies where there are anti-miscegenation laws, it is argued, may lead to a craving for that which is mysterious and prohibited. Thus, interracial relationships are destined to take on a predominantly fetishised form in which there is little likelihood of an authentic meeting of persons. Similarly, Gill (1995) suggests that sexual attraction forms the base of the relationship because the couple are more attracted by the sexual chemistry and the alluring promise it portends.

5. Revenge for racial and social oppression. This explanation, which has its roots in the radical black politics of the 1960s and 1970s, advances the view that black men are involved in interracial relationships as a form of vindictiveness and vindication. In making this case Elridge Cleaver (1968) argued that, as a result of the historical legacy of slavery, colonialism, racial discrimination and social oppression, black men may become involved in interracial relationships as a means of avenging the injustices, degradation and oppression that has befallen not just them as individuals but black people as a race. In this account, the interracial relationship is the forum in which black men demonstrate to white men that they now have the social and sexual power to appropriate their most prized possession, white women. Moreover, having appropriated the white woman, they proceed to defile 'it' thus asserting their mastery, as men, once more.

6. Geographical propinquity and shortage of same race partner. Kannan (1973), Sister Lynn (1953) and Kennedy (1943) all maintained that as black and white people find themselves sharing the same social space in a situation where same race partners were in short supply, they would inevitably develop intimate relationships.

7. Mutual affection and shared interests. This explanation is seldom advanced by critics of interracial relationships, not least one suspects because it suggests that they might have a great deal in common with same-race relationships (Duck, 1993).

This list is of course not exhaustive, but they represent the major popular and scholarly explanations of the motivations of people forming intimate interracial relationships. Whether real or illusory, these assertions often provide the backdrop against which attitudes towards, and approaches to, working with mixed parentage children and their families are developed by welfare professionals.

A guide to this book

This volume is intended for social work practitioners, students, academics, trainers, foster carers and adopters as well as those interested in the lives of and experiences of children of mixed (interracial) parentage. The aim of this volume is not to patronise practitioners by producing an uncomplicated ready-made, 'how-to', step-by-step guide. This point was made clearly during a private conversation with the social work academic Ravi Kholi who warned against yet another publication that *presumes* to offer easy solutions to practitioners without taking account of their depth of knowledge and understanding of the issues involved or of producing a book that fails to take account of their experiences. In the light of this warning, this volume assumes that some practitioners may well be aware of some of the issues but that many may need to review these in the light of the debates and the research findings contained within it. This book does contain 'messages' for practitioners but they are complex ones which must be filtered through the knowledge, skills and practice wisdom of individual practitioners. There is also a difficulty associated with offering guidelines to policy makers who are charged with the responsibility of ensuring that services meet the needs of the families and children who are the subjects of this book. There are no simplistic policy guidelines to be derived from these pages but there is a plea to policy makers to open up a space where a thoughtful and innovative practice can be developed with mixed parentage children and their families.

The contributors to this volume, most of whom are, or have been, practitioners in this field, are at the cutting edge of theory and practice in the area of mixed race families and their children in the UK and are therefore able to offer both an insightful analysis of the problems and grounded suggestions and directions for action.

This introductory chapter has attempted to contextualise the experiences of children of mixed parentage by exploring popular and scholarly perceptions of the motivations of those entering interracial relationships, suggesting that unless the realities of the lives of those involved in interracial relationships is examined in depth, there is a danger that this discourse is likely to have a negative impact upon the perceptions of professionals and policy makers.

In Chapter 2 Charlie Owen discusses how the 'mixed race' categories in the census have evolved and, drawing upon recent census data charts the growth and geographical spread of mixed parentage families in the UK. He then provides an incisive analysis of the implications of these changes for future policy and practice.

In Chapter 3 Owusu-Bempah provides an historical analysis of attitudes towards interracial relationships and the children born of such relationships. In his measured dissection of the arguments, he asks for a reflective approach and for practitioners to think about the damaging effects that racial beliefs, assumptions and stereotypes may have on practice and, consequently, on the children. He argues that there is a need for greater awareness of the damage that is inflicted upon the children's psychological functioning, as well as their life-chances, as a result of denying them self-definition.

Ilan Katz and Amal Treacher, in Chapter 4, argue that there seems to be little room to address the complexity and diversity experienced by mixed race children. They explore the current debates about 'mixed race (or biracial or dual heritage or mixed parentage) children, 'identity' and 'development', and attempt to advance the debate within social work.

Chapter 5 builds on the work of Katz and Treacher, arguing that, even as practitioners may attempt to redress the social inequalities that exist between black and white people in society at large, the approach taken towards children of mixed parentage often ignores half of the child's background. Taking their cues from what they see as the racist 'one drop rule', they account for the reluctance of many progressives involved in this field to move away from a binary worldview and embrace a more fluid and evolutionary conception of identity.

Lena Robinson, in Chapter 6, argues that monoracial models of minority identity development do not address all the issues facing children of mixed-parentage. And she goes on to identify the ways in which practitioners can extend their knowledge and understanding and enhance their effectiveness in their work with children of mixed parentage.

In Chapter 7 Annabel Goodyer argues that social work's response to mixed race children has a history of using simplistic interpretations in complex situations. Drawing upon a range of theoretical perspectives, including those developed within anthropology, she suggests ways in which existing provision can be adapted to meet the needs of children of mixed parentage.

The experiences of white mothers of children of mixed parentage is often ignored or subsumed within the discussion of their children and their experiences. Vicki Harman and Ravinder Barn rectify this omission by exploring the discourses concerning the white mothers of mixed race children in Chapter 8.

The findings from a follow-up study of children of mixed race parentage placed with permanent substitute families in the early 1980s are the focus of June Thoburn's discussion in Chapter 9. Here she demonstrates that physical appearance and the culture, religion and country of origin of the kinship group (a child's 'heritage') are important components of identity but she also asserts that the geographical, social class and emotional environment in which a child grows up interact with heritage in contributing to an adult sense of self and self esteem. Her analysis indicates that children of mixed parentage are more likely to wait longer in care before being adopted by families of similar heritage; remain in unplanned and often unstable care; or be placed with families whose appearance and culture differ significantly from those of their birth families. She also reveals that children of mixed parentage are less likely to have continuing contact with their families of origin than other children in the care system.

Chapter 10 examines the contexts in which children of mixed parentage develop and the everyday perceptions that 'others' have about them. In this chapter Gillian Olumide draws out some tentative ways of thinking about the disproportionate representation of mixed race children in the public care system. She highlights ways in which this question might be addressed within the social work constituency along with the appropriate treatment of children.

Conclusion

Taken together these chapters offer the practitioner and the policy maker the means to develop a practice with mixed race children and young people which could enable them to develop a positive sense of self and their own definition of their identity. Beyond this, however, it also suggests how the adults around them might begin to break out of the confines of a binary worldview imposed by an uninformed set of assumptions.

References

Alibhai-Brown, Y. and Montague, A. (1992) *The Colour of Love: Mixed Race Relationships.* London: Virago.

Alibhai-Brown, Y. (2001) *Mixed Feelings: The Complex Lives of Mixed-Race Britons.* London: Women's Press.

Banks, N. (1992) Techniques for Direct Work with Black Children. *Fostering and Adoption.* 16: 3, 19–25.

Banks, N. (1995) Children of Black Mixed Parentage and their Placement Needs. *Fostering and Adoption.* 19: 2, 19–24.

Bastide, R. (1961) Dusky Venus, Black Apollo, in Baxter, P. and Sansom, B. (1972). *Race and Social Difference.* Harmondsworth: Penguin.

Cleaver, E. (1968) *Soul on Ice.* New York: McGraw-Hill.

Duck, S. (Ed.) (1993) *Social Context of Relationships.* California: Sage.

Fanon, F. (1952) *Black Skin, White Mask.* London: Pluto Press.

Ferguson, I.L. (1982) *Fantastic Experiences of a Half-Blind, and his Interracial Marriage.* San-Francisco: Lunan-Ferguson.

Fryer, P. (1984) *Staying Power.* London: Pluto.

Gill, A. (1995) *Ruling Passion. Race, Sex and Empire.* London: BBC.

Henriques, F. (1975) *Children of Conflict: A Study of Interracial Sex and Marriage.* New York: Dutton Press.

Jones, C., Lavallette, M. and Penketh, L. (1998) *Anti-Racism and Social Welfare.* England: Ashgate.

Kannan, C.T. (1973) *Interracial Marriages in London, A Comparative Study.* London: CT Press.

Katz, I. (1996) *The Construction of Racial Identity in Children of Mixed Parentage: A Mixed Metaphor.* London: JKP.

Kennedy, R.J.S. (1943) *Pre-marital Residential Propinquity and Ethnic Endogamy.* AJS XLVIII.

Maximé, J.E. (1993) The Importance of Racial Identity for the Psychological Well-Being of Black Children. *Association for Child Psychology and Psychiatry Review and Newsletter.* 15: 4.

Modood, T., Berthoud, R., Lakey, J., Nazroo, J.Y., Smith, P. et al. (1997) *Ethnic Minorities in Britain.* London: Policy Studies Institute.

Olumide, G. (2002) *Raiding the Gene Pool: The Social Construction of Mixed Race.* London: Pluto.

Parker, D. and Song, M. (Eds.) (2001) *Rethinking Mixed Race.* London: Pluto Press.

Phoenix, A. and Tizard, B. (1993) *Black, White or Mixed Race: Race and Racism in the Lives of Young People of Mixed Parentage.* London: Routledge.

Prevatt-Goldstein, B. (1999) Direct Work with Black Children with One White Parent, in Barn, R. (Ed.) *Working with Black Children and Adolescents in Need.* London: BAAF.

Shahrazad, Ali. (1989) *The Black Man's Guide to Understanding the Black Woman.* Califonia: SA Press.

Sister, Lynn. (1953) *Intermarriages in Washington DC 1940–47.* Washington: Catholic University Press.

Small, J. (1986) Transracial Placement: Conflict and Contradiction, in Ahmed, S., Cheetham, J. and Small, J. (Eds.) (1986) *Social Work with Black Children and Their Families.* London: Batsford.

Wade, P. (1993) *Blackness and Race Mixture: The Dynamics of Racial Identity in Colombia.* USA: John Hopkins University Press.

Warren, M.D. and Johnson, W.R. (Eds.) (1994) *Inside the Mixed Marriage: Account of Changing Attitudes, Patterns, and Perception of Cross-Cultural and Interracial Marriage.* New York: UPA.

Chapter 2

Looking at Numbers and Projections: Making Sense of the Census and Emerging Trends

Charlie Owen

Introduction: Origins of the census question

The first time an ethnic question was included in a British census was in 1991. Extensive testing of a possible ethnic question had been conducted prior to the 1981 census, but in the end the government decided not to include a question. Some tested versions included an option of ticking more than one category: these versions 'instructed the form-filler to 'tick all the boxes that apply', if the person was of mixed ancestry. However, we found that multi-ticking was unreliable' (Sillitoe, 1978: 17). Other versions included a separate category of 'mixed', but this too was rejected, despite the successful inclusion of such a category in the ethnic question for the Labour Force Survey (LFS) since its instigation in 1973. The recommended version resulting from these tests included a final box with the following caption: Any other race or ethnic group, or if of mixed racial or ethnic descent (please describe below). However, even this was acknowledged as unsatisfactory, as it would not always be possible to distinguish, on the basis of the written answers, people of 'mixed' origin from those of an ethnicity 'other' than those listed in the question: 'we shall have just to reconcile ourselves to some undercounting of people of mixed ancestry, if a question of this kind is used in the Census' (Sillitoe, 1978: 19)

Further tests were conducted prior to the 1991 census, as 'The recording of mixed descent had always been unsatisfactory in our previous tests' (Sillitoe, 1981: 12). The team from the Office for Population Censuses and Surveys (OPCS) acknowledged the success of the LFS question, with a single 'mixed' category, but chose a different strategy: 'In our previous tests, we tried a variety of methods of recording the ethnic identity of such persons, but with little success…therefore, we abandoned the attempt to classify all persons of mixed descent in the same way, and simply added an instruction to the question which reads, 'If the person is descended from more than one group, please tick the one to which the person considers he or she belongs, or…describe the person's ancestry in the space provided' (Sillitoe, 1987: 3–5).

It was a slightly modified version of this wording that was adopted for the 1991 census: 'If the person is descended from more than one ethnic or racial group, please tick the group to which the person considers he/she belongs, or tick the 'Any other ethnic group' box and describe the person's ancestry in the space provided'. So there was no specific category of 'mixed' to tick. Instead people who wanted to identify as 'mixed' were encouraged to choose a single category, or failing that to write a description. There were nine boxes for the question, and two of them included space for a written answer: these were the boxes for 'black-Other' and 'Any other ethnic group'. On the basis of these written answers OPCS developed a more detailed ethnic categorisation than the nine tick boxes: coders were given detailed instructions on how to assign these written answers to 35 categories. The procedure is described by Bulmer (1996), (see also Owen (2001) for more detail).

The more detailed classification from these written answers included three mixed categories that will be examined in some detail here; these are 'black/white', 'Asian/white' and 'Other Mixed'. (There was also a category of 'Mixed white', but I am not considering that in this chapter.)

1991 census

Only one table was ever published using the full ethnic group classification. This is Table A in the census volume *1991 Census: Ethnic Group and Country of Birth, Great Britain* (OPCS/GRO(S), 1993). This table consists of a head count at district level. However, there is no further detail. In particular, no information of the age distribution of the mixed groups was ever published. I commissioned a special table from OPCS. This table gives a population count for the full 35-way ethnic group classification, broken down into 5-year age bands, but with no subdivisions for area. Instead, the table just gives a single count for Great Britain.

Table 1 shows the counts for the three mixed categories. The total is 228,504, made up of 54,569 classified as 'Mixed: black/white' (23.9 per cent of total mixed), 61,874 'Mixed: Asian/white' (27.1 per cent), and 112,061 'Other Mixed' (49.0 per cent). It is notable that the 'other' category is almost as large as the other two categories combined. However, this probably says more about how the classification was applied than about the constitution of the population. Remember, these were not boxes that census takers could tick, but were derived from their written answers: anyone who wrote 'mixed race' or 'mixed parentage' was assigned to the 'other' category, as was anyone who wrote 'half-caste'. Obviously, many of the people assigned to 'other' would have been assigned to one of the more detailed categories if they had given more detail. Consequently we cannot draw any firm conclusions about the make up of the overall 'mixed' population as identified in the 1991 census: it is, therefore, safer to consider just the total mixed.

These figures are also shown graphically in Figure 1. The most striking feature of this graph is the very skewed age distribution of the mixed population. The last column of

Table 1: Numbers identified as mixed: Census 1991: Great Britain

	Mixed: black/white	Mixed: Asian/white	Other Mixed	Total	Percentage
0–4	14,309	10,281	28,961	53,551	23.4
5–9	10,145	8,078	20,827	39,050	17.1
10–14	7,098	6,382	14,087	27,567	12.1
15–19	5,594	5,622	10,292	21,508	9.4
20–24	5,114	5,768	9,640	20,522	9.0
25–29	4,808	5,380	8,966	19,154	8.4
30–34	3,113	3,744	5,887	12,744	5.6
45–39	1,564	2,890	3,524	7,978	3.5
40–44	872	2,613	2,699	6,184	2.7
45–49	636	2,134	2,076	4,846	2.1
50–54	356	2,065	1,500	3,921	1.7
55–59	283	1,906	1,195	3,384	1.5
60–64	245	1,752	961	2,958	1.3
65–69	182	1,321	639	2,142	0.9
70–74	123	910	392	1,425	0.6
75–79	59	562	207	828	0.4
80–84	37	290	122	449	0.2
85+	31	176	86	293	0.1
Total	54,569	61,874	112,061	228,504	100

Source: Specially commissioned table

Table 1 shows the percentage of the total mixed population in each of the age bands. Almost a quarter (23.4 per cent), were children aged under 5. By contrast, just 6.6 per cent of the total population were in this youngest age band. Taking the first three age bands together, more than half (52.6 per cent), of the mixed population were children aged under 15. This compares to 18.9 per cent in the total population. At the other end of the age scale, just 2.2 per cent of the mixed population were aged 65 and over, compared to 16.1 per cent of the total population. Clearly, the mixed population was much younger than the overall population. Table 2 shows the mixed groups and the total mixed as a percentage of the total population within each age band. Overall, the mixed population was less than half of one per cent of the total population (0.42 per cent). However, because of the skewed age distribution, it formed a much larger percentage of the total population at the younger ages. For the youngest age group, zero to four, the mixed population formed almost one and a half per cent of the total population (1.47 per cent). Bear in mind that in the 1991 census 94.5 per cent of the population were classified as white. This implies that the mixed populations formed 7.6 per cent of the minority ethnic population: among the under-5s, they were 16.0 per cent. This shows that, whilst quite small as a percentage of the total population, the mixed groups were becoming a significant percentage of the minority ethnic population of

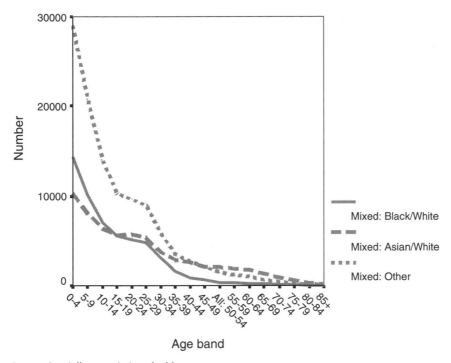

Source: Specially commissioned table

Figure 1: Numbers identified as mixed by age band: Census 1991: Great Britain

Great Britain, especially at the younger ages. Taking all ages together, the mixed total exceeds the total black African, Bangladeshi and Chinese populations; among the under-5s only the Indian and Pakistani ethnic groups exceeded the mixed population.

There was considerable dissatisfaction with the quality of the data on the mixed populations from the 1991 census. It was widely believed to be a significant under-count, because there was no category of mixed – and the instructions encouraged people who wanted to identify as mixed to tick just one box: One suggestion is that many people who would have identified as mixed simply ticked the 'black other' box (Owen, 1996), and so did not get counted as mixed. Secondly, if people wrote some-thing that was not recognised as 'mixed', then they would have been assigned to one of the other categories. That this could easily happen is shown by examining the instructions to data coders. For example, 'English West Indian would imply non-mixed, but English and West Indian would imply mixed origin' (Extract from OPCS internal document: Supervisor Coding Instructions for Ethnic Group). There is some direct evidence for the census giving an undercount: the LFS ethnic question included a specific category of mixed, so people could choose that directly. After 1991, the

Table 2: Percentage in each age band identified as mixed: Census 1991: Great Britain

	Mixed: black/white	Mixed: Asian/white	Other Mixed	Total
0–4	0.39	0.28	0.80	1.47
5–9	0.29	0.23	0.61	1.14
10–14	0.22	0.19	0.43	0.84
15–19	0.16	0.16	0.29	0.61
20–24	0.12	0.14	0.23	0.50
25–29	0.11	0.12	0.21	0.44
30–34	0.08	0.09	0.15	0.32
45–39	0.04	0.08	0.10	0.22
40–44	0.02	0.07	0.07	0.15
45–49	0.02	0.06	0.06	0.14
50–54	0.01	0.07	0.05	0.13
55–59	0.01	0.07	0.04	0.12
60–64	0.01	0.06	0.03	0.10
65–69	0.01	0.05	0.02	0.08
70–74	0.01	0.04	0.02	0.06
75–79	0.00	0.03	0.01	0.05
80–84	0.00	0.02	0.01	0.04
85+	0.00	0.02	0.01	0.04
Total	0.10	0.11	0.20	0.42

Source: Specially commissioned table

question was changed to match the census question. Nevertheless, it is possible to compare the census estimate of the mixed population with the LFS estimate prior to the change. I added data for the first quarter of 1989, 1990 and 1991. (It is necessary to combine three years in order to get a sufficiently large sample.) The LFS estimate was that all mixed groups combined formed 0.52 per cent of the total population, compared to an estimate of 0.42 per cent from the census (Phoenix and Owen, 1996).

2001 census

Following the 1991 census there were further consultations on the ethnic question in preparation for the 2001 census. Partly as a result of the problems identified above in the 1991 counts for mixed groups, partly in recognition of the growing demographic significance of the mixed population, and also partly in recognition of the wish of many people from mixed backgrounds to be able to identify themselves as such, it was agreed that explicit categories of 'mixed' would be included in the ethnic question on the 2001 census (see Aspinall, 1996). The final wording for the census in England and Wales included the following:

Mixed

- White and black Caribbean
- White and black African
- White and Asian
- Any other mixed background. Please describe:

The ethnic questions in Scotland and in Northern Ireland were slightly different. In particular, they each had only a single mixed category, without the more detailed sub-categories. This means that data from different parts of the United Kingdom are not directly comparable. Moreover, data for England and Wales are published together, using the same formats; data for Scotland and for Northern Ireland are each published separately and the data on ethnic groups have been published using different age bands. Furthermore, these age bands are not evenly spaced. It is possible, never-theless, to combine the data from the different data files to give one consistent dataset. This is shown in Table 3.

The 2001 census estimates that, in the United Kingdom, there were 677,118 people who identified as 'mixed' by choosing one of the mixed categories for the ethnic question. The figure for Great Britain was 673,798: this almost three times the figure recorded in 1991, an increase of 195 per cent. Some of this apparent growth will be due to the undercount in 1991, but most of it is likely to reflect a real growth in the mixed population, reflecting its young age profile in 1991. (Even taking the larger LFS estimate of the mixed population for 1991, the mixed population had increased by 138 per cent in 2001). Over the same period, the total population of Great Britain had increased by just 4.0 per cent.

Table 3: Numbers identifying as Mixed: Census 2001: United Kingdom

	England	Wales	Scotland	Great Britain	Northern Ireland	United Kingdom
0 to 4	113,540	2,657	1,895	118,092	636	118,728
5 to 9	101,085	2,575	1,719	105,379	518	105,897
10 to 14	91,680	2,555	1,737	95,972	501	96,473
15 to 19	69,633	1,965	1,469	73,067	365	73,432
20 to 24	50,448	1,376	1,351	53,175	220	53,395
25 to 34	88,148	2,110	1,768	92,026	416	92,442
35 to 44	64,375	1,861	1,117	67,353	315	67,668
45 to 59	38,400	1,457	922	40,779	182	40,961
60 to 64	7,508	293	183	7,984	53	8,037
65 to 74	10,861	462	338	11,661	63	11,724
75 to 84	5,795	281	206	6,282	42	6,324
85+	1,900	69	59	2,028	9	2,037
Total	643,373	17,661	12,764	673,798	3,320	677,118

Table 4: Percentage within each age band identifying as Mixed: Census 2001: United Kingdom

	England	Wales	Scotland	Great Britain	Northern Ireland	United Kingdom
0 to 4	3.88	1.58	0.68	3.50	0.55	3.41
5 to 9	3.24	1.39	0.56	2.92	0.42	2.83
10 to 14	2.84	1.30	0.54	2.56	0.38	2.49
15 to 19	2.30	1.06	0.46	2.07	0.28	2.00
20 to 24	1.71	0.81	0.43	1.55	0.20	1.51
25 to 34	1.25	0.58	0.25	1.13	0.17	1.11
35 to 44	0.88	0.46	0.14	0.79	0.13	0.77
45 to 59	0.41	0.26	0.09	0.38	0.06	0.37
60 to 64	0.31	0.19	0.07	0.28	0.07	0.28
65 to 74	0.26	0.17	0.08	0.24	0.05	0.24
75 to 84	0.21	0.15	0.08	0.20	0.05	0.19
85+	0.20	0.12	0.07	0.18	0.04	0.18
Total	1.31	0.61	0.25	1.18	0.20	1.15

In percentage terms, the mixed population in the United Kingdom constituted 1.15 per cent of the total population of 58,789,187. The figure for Great Britain was 1.18 per cent of 57,103,927, up from 0.42 per cent in 1991 – almost three times. This was an increase of 181 per cent (or 127 per cent on the LFS estimate for 1991). In 2001 the mixed population constituted 14.6 per cent of the minority population, nearly double what it was in 1991.

England and Wales

More detail is available for England and Wales than for the rest of the United Kingdom, both in terms of the number of mixed categories and the finer detail of age, so the rest of this chapter will present data only for England and Wales.

The question in England and Wales had four categories under the heading 'Mixed', and data are available for all four categories. A detailed age breakdown, into 5-year age bands is shown in Table 5. It is clear that the largest of the mixed groups was the 'white and black Caribbean' group. They numbered 237,420, or 35.9 per cent of all people who identified as mixed. Next was 'white and Asian' at 189,015 or 28.6 per cent of all mixed. 'white and black African' were 78,911 or 11.9 per cent. The final group of 'Other Mixed' was larger, at 155,688 (23.6 per cent): unless the Office for National Statistics publishes an analysis of the written answers for this 'Other' group, it will be difficult to know quite who is included.

The data are also shown in Figure 2. This shows a similar pattern to the graph for the 1991 census, Figure 1. That is, the numbers are much higher among the younger

Table 5: Numbers in categories of mixed: Census 2001: England and Wales

	Mixed: white and black Caribbean	Mixed: white and black African	Mixed: white and Asian	Mixed: Other Mixed	Total
0 to 4	44,985	14,310	32,521	24,381	116,197
5 to 9	44,065	10,987	27,677	20,931	103,660
10 to 14	40,766	8,993	25,020	19,456	94,235
15 to 19	27,965	7,221	19,951	16,461	71,598
20 to 24	16,654	6,584	15,116	13,470	51,824
25 to 29	13,434	6,231	13,388	11,939	44,992
30 to 34	13,966	6,391	13,522	11,387	45,266
35 to 39	12,429	5,632	11,724	9,795	39,580
40 to 44	7,526	4,344	7,655	7,131	26,656
45 to 49	3,462	2,831	5,377	5,404	17,074
50 to 54	2,607	1,715	4,393	4,466	13,181
55 to 59	2,003	1,107	3,279	3,213	9,602
60 to 64	1,955	793	2,744	2,309	7,801
65 to 69	1,693	607	2,267	1,713	6,280
70 to 74	1,471	438	1,799	1,335	5,043
75 to 79	1,073	327	1,311	1,009	3,720
80 to 84	722	220	708	706	2,356
85 to 89	394	113	368	387	1,262
90+	250	67	195	195	707
Total	237,420	78,911	189,015	155,688	661,034

age groups. This is shown more clearly in Table 6, which shows, within each of mixed categories, the percentage of the group in each age band. Taking the total mixed population, over 17 per cent were children aged under 5: this percentage was slightly higher for the 'white and black Caribbean' group (18.95 per cent), and the 'white and black African' group (18.13 per cent). This compares with just 5.95 per cent in this age band for all people (the final column of Table 6). In fact, the percentages in each 5-year age band are fairly consistent in this column, at around six to seven per cent (They gradually fall off after the age of 60). This pattern of equal percentages in each 5-year band is what would be expected in a stable population, not growing through higher numbers of births. The pattern for each of the mixed groups is quite different: they all show much higher percentages amongst children and young people. Indeed, almost half (47.52 per cent) of the mixed population were children aged under-15, whereas for all people the corresponding percentage was under one-fifth (18.89 per cent). The pattern is most extreme for the 'white and black Caribbean' group, where more than half of the group were under-15 (54.68 per cent). At older ages the percentage for each of the mixed groups is much smaller (This is shown clearly in

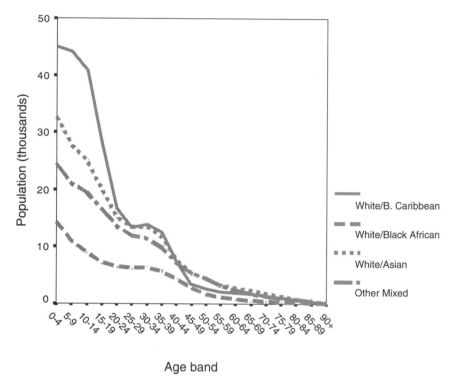

Figure 2: Numbers identified as mixed by age band: Census 2001: England and Wales

Figure 3). This figure also shows the remarkable similarity in the age profile for the different mixed groups.

Another way of considering the data is in terms of what percentage of all people are in each mixed group. This is shown in Table 7: although this looks like Table 6, in Table 7 the percentages within an age band sum to 100, whereas in Table 6 it is the percentages within each mixed group that sum to 100. Taking the total row, at the bottom of the table, it can be seen that 1.27 per cent of the total population in 2001 were classified, by their answers to the census question, as mixed. This compares to an estimate of 0.42 per cent from the 1991 census. As explained above, this was certainly an underestimate; nevertheless, this is still a very big increase in just ten years. Of course, because of the young age profile of the mixed groups compared to the overall population, the percentage of the population who are mixed is higher at the younger ages. As can be seen in Table 7, almost four per cent of all under-5s in England and Wales in 2001 were mixed (3.76 per cent). This is still quite a small percentage. But remember, in the 2001 census, 91 per cent of the population were identified as 'white': the mixed group as a

Table 6: Percentage within each mixed category in each age band: Census 2001: England and Wales

	Mixed: white and black Caribbean	Mixed: white and black African	Mixed: white and Asian	Mixed: Other Mixed	Mixed: Total	All People
0 to 4	18.95	18.13	17.21	15.66	17.58	5.95
5 to 9	18.56	13.92	14.64	13.44	15.68	6.36
10 to 14	17.17	11.40	13.24	12.50	14.26	6.58
15 to 19	11.78	9.15	10.56	10.57	10.83	6.18
20 to 24	7.01	8.34	8.00	8.65	7.84	6.00
25 to 29	5.66	7.90	7.08	7.67	6.81	6.60
30 to 34	5.88	8.10	7.15	7.31	6.85	7.66
35 to 39	5.24	7.14	6.20	6.29	5.99	7.87
40 to 44	3.17	5.50	4.05	4.58	4.03	7.03
45 to 49	1.46	3.59	2.84	3.47	2.58	6.33
50 to 54	1.10	2.17	2.32	2.87	1.99	6.90
55 to 59	0.84	1.40	1.73	2.06	1.45	5.69
60 to 64	0.82	1.00	1.45	1.48	1.18	4.89
65 to 69	0.71	0.77	1.20	1.10	0.95	4.41
70 to 74	0.62	0.56	0.95	0.86	0.76	3.99
75 to 79	0.45	0.41	0.69	0.65	0.56	3.37
80 to 84	0.30	0.28	0.37	0.45	0.36	2.26
85 to 89	0.17	0.14	0.19	0.25	0.19	1.30
90+	0.11	0.08	0.10	0.13	0.11	0.65
Total	100	100	100	100	100	100

percentage of the rest, the minority ethnic population, is much larger. Overall, the percentage of the minority ethnic population that is mixed was 14.6: of the minority ethnic under-5 population, the mixed groups made up over a quarter (26.2 per cent).

In 2001, one and a quarter per cent of all people in England and Wales were of mixed origin: one sixth of the minority ethnic population were of mixed origin. Almost four per cent of all under-5s in England and Wales were of mixed origin: one quarter of the minority ethnic population of under-5s were of mixed origin. This is a huge demographic shift in the population. What is most striking is not so much the growth of the mixed populations as a percentage of the total population – but as a percentage of the minority ethnic population.

Minority ethnic population

There is no necessity why a growth in the mixed population should be more rapid than the growth of the minority ethnic population in general, but that is what is

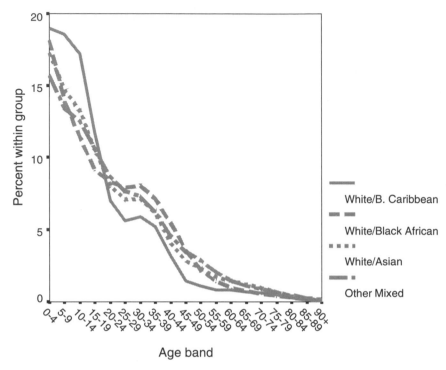

Figure 3: Percentage within each mixed category in each age band: Census 2001: England and Wales

happening. Table 8 shows the numbers in three of the mixed groups alongside the ethnic group that is mixed with white in the 'mixed' category. So 'black Caribbean' is next to 'Mixed: white and black Caribbean'; 'black African' is next to 'Mixed: white and black African'; 'Asian' is next to 'Mixed: white and Asian'. ('Asian' here is the sum of four columns in the main census tables: 'Indian', 'Pakistani', 'Bangladeshi' and 'Other Asian'.) These same figures are shown in Table 9: the mixed group is shown as a percentage of the adjacent main ethnic group. (NB: The mixed group is not *part of* the main minority ethnic group: the percentage shows the groups' relative sizes. A percentage of 100 would indicate that there were equal numbers in the mixed group and the main group).

The 'white and Asian' group is the smallest relative to the main Asian group, 8.31 per cent. The percentage is highest among the younger age groups, with the mixed group equal to 15.59 per cent of the Asian under-5 group. Another way of reading this is that for every six Asian children under the age of five, there was one mixed white and Asian child of the same age. There is a curious increase in the percentage in the later years: after age 64 the percentage in the mixed group relative to the Asian group

Table 7: Percentage within each age band in each mixed category: Census 2001: England and Wales

	Mixed: white and black Caribbean	Mixed: white and black African	Mixed: white and Asian	Mixed: Other Mixed	Mixed: Total	All People
0 to 4	1.45	0.46	1.05	0.79	3.76	100
5 to 9	1.33	0.33	0.84	0.63	3.13	100
10 to 14	1.19	0.26	0.73	0.57	2.75	100
15 to 19	0.87	0.22	0.62	0.51	2.23	100
20 to 24	0.53	0.21	0.48	0.43	1.66	100
25 to 29	0.39	0.18	0.39	0.35	1.31	100
30 to 34	0.35	0.16	0.34	0.29	1.14	100
35 to 39	0.30	0.14	0.29	0.24	0.97	100
40 to 44	0.21	0.12	0.21	0.20	0.73	100
45 to 49	0.11	0.09	0.16	0.16	0.52	100
50 to 54	0.07	0.05	0.12	0.12	0.37	100
55 to 59	0.07	0.04	0.11	0.11	0.32	100
60 to 64	0.08	0.03	0.11	0.09	0.31	100
65 to 69	0.07	0.03	0.10	0.07	0.27	100
70 to 74	0.07	0.02	0.09	0.06	0.24	100
75 to 79	0.06	0.02	0.07	0.06	0.21	100
80 to 84	0.06	0.02	0.06	0.06	0.20	100
85 to 89	0.06	0.02	0.05	0.06	0.19	100
90+	0.07	0.02	0.06	0.06	0.21	100
Total	0.46	0.15	0.36	0.30	1.27	100

increases fairly steadily with age. However, this trend is based on fairly small numbers, especially in the oldest age bands.

The 'Mixed: white and black African' group is larger relative to the 'black African' group: overall the percentage is 16.45. As with the mixed white and Asian group, this mixed group shows higher percentages at both the younger and the older ages. In fact the highest relative percentage is for the 85 to 89 age band. However, at the older ages the trend is based on even smaller numbers. Nevertheless, it is interesting that this group shows the same trend. The numbers are higher for the younger ages, so the percentages are more reliable. Taking the youngest group, the under-5s, the mixed are equivalent to 28.16 per cent of the black African group – more than a quarter.

Finally, to the 'Mixed: white and black Caribbean' group as a percentage of the 'black Caribbean' group. Overall the percentage is 42.11. This group shows the same rise in percentage at older ages: among the group 90 and over the percentage of mixed relative to the main group was 42.11 – almost half. As before, at the older ages the percentages are based on quite small numbers, but it is interesting that all three

Table 8: Mixed and main minority ethnic groups by age band: Census 2001: England and Wales

	Black Caribbean	Mixed: white and black Caribbean	Black African	Mixed: white and black African	Asian	Mixed: white and Asian
0 to 4	32,205	44,985	50,815	14,310	208,557	32,521
5 to 9	35,759	44,065	46,402	10,987	200,093	27,677
10 to 14	38,925	40,766	39,898	8,993	201,451	25,020
15 to 19	37,625	27,965	38,964	7,221	215,147	19,951
20 to 24	30,987	16,654	38,593	6,584	219,749	15,116
25 to 29	34,524	13,434	47,201	6,231	216,779	13,388
30 to 34	57,875	13,966	60,788	6,391	203,780	13,522
35 to 39	74,429	12,429	53,327	5,632	160,051	11,724
40 to 44	53,796	7,526	37,931	4,344	154,881	7,655
45 to 49	32,084	3,462	22,105	2,831	138,914	5,377
50 to 54	20,742	2,607	14,553	1,715	97,103	4,393
55 to 59	23,539	2,003	9,637	1,107	67,782	3,279
60 to 64	31,491	1,955	8,319	793	69,390	2,744
65 to 69	26,664	1,693	4,936	607	52,638	2,267
70 to 74	17,777	1,471	2,929	438	33,041	1,799
75 to 79	9,136	1,073	1,648	327	17,888	1,311
80 to 84	4,111	722	1,021	220	10,345	708
85 to 89	1,474	394	360	113	3,837	368
90+	700	250	238	67	2,311	195
Total	563,843	237,420	479,665	78,911	2,273,737	189,015

groups show higher percentages of mixed (relative to the main ethnic group) at the older ages. However, the high percentage at the younger ages is even more pronounced here. Indeed, for each of the three age bands 0 to 4, 5 to 9 and 10 to 14 there were more children of mixed white and black Caribbean origin than of black Caribbean origin. Looked at another way, taking all children who had at least one black Caribbean parent, there were more where the second parent was white than where the second parent was also black Caribbean.

Location

So far percentages for the whole of England and Wales have been considered. However, the mixed populations are not evenly spread. The percentage in the local population for administrative areas (county districts, unitary authorities, metropolitan districts and London boroughs) for all mixed groups combined and all ages vary from 4.83 for Lambeth in Inner London to 0.15 for Alnwick, Northumberland. The top 30 areas are shown in Table 10. All of the top ten are in inner London; the next four are in

Table 9: Mixed as a percentage of main minority ethnic groups by age band: Census 2001: England and Wales

	Mixed: white and black Caribbean as percentage of black Caribbean	Mixed: white and black African as percentage of black African	Mixed: white and Asian as percentage of Asian
0 to 4	139.68	28.16	15.59
5 to 9	123.23	23.68	13.83
10 to 14	104.73	22.54	12.42
15 to 19	74.33	18.53	9.27
20 to 24	53.75	17.06	6.88
25 to 29	38.91	13.20	6.18
30 to 34	24.13	10.51	6.64
35 to 39	16.70	10.56	7.33
40 to 44	13.99	11.45	4.94
45 to 49	10.79	12.81	3.87
50 to 54	12.57	11.78	4.52
55 to 59	8.51	11.49	4.84
60 to 64	6.21	9.53	3.95
65 to 69	6.35	12.30	4.31
70 to 74	8.27	14.95	5.44
75 to 79	11.74	19.84	7.33
80 to 84	17.56	21.55	6.84
85 to 89	26.73	31.39	9.59
90+	35.71	28.15	8.44
Total	42.11	16.45	8.31

outer London, and then two more inner London. Number 17 is the metropolitan district of Manchester, with the highest percentage outside London. Next comes Nottingham unitary authority. Four more outer London areas, then the metropolitan district of Birmingham, in the West Midlands; two more outer London then Wolverhampton, also in the West Midlands. Next comes Luton, then an inner London borough, an outer London one and the Forest Heath district of Suffolk. This last may seem anomalous, but the high percentage may be linked to the military bases of Mildenhall and Lakenheath, both of which are in this district.

In the top 30 are 24 London boroughs (out of a total of 33), three metropolitan districts and two urban unitary authorities. This suggests strongly that the mixed population is concentrated in urban areas generally and London in particular.

The same table could be presented for each of the mixed groups, but the results are very similar in each case, with London making up the bulk of the top 30. This further suggests that the different mixed groups might also be found in the same areas. This is confirmed by the pattern of correlations shown in Table 11. These show

Table 10: Administrative areas by percent mixed: top 30

Rank	Percent	Area	Within
1	4.83	Lambeth	Inner London
2	4.55	Harringey	Inner London
3	4.19	Hackney	Inner London
4	4.18	Lewisham	Inner London
5	4.13	Westminster	Inner London
6	4.11	Islington	Inner London
7	4.09	Kensington and Chelsea	Inner London
8	3.82	Hammersmith and Fulham	Inner London
9	3.75	Camden	Inner London
10	3.73	Southwark	Inner London
11	3.72	Brent	Outer London
12	3.72	Croydon	Outer London
13	3.62	Ealing	Outer London
14	3.55	Waltham Forest	Outer London
15	3.38	Newham	Inner London
16	3.35	Wandsworth	Inner London
17	3.23	Manchester	Greater Manchester
18	3.13	Nottingham	
19	3.13	Merton	Outer London
20	3.04	Hounslow	Outer London
21	3.02	Barnet	Outer London
22	2.96	Enfield	Outer London
23	2.86	Birmingham	West Midlands
24	2.82	Harrow	Outer London
25	2.74	Greenwich	Outer London
26	2.72	Wolverhampton	West Midlands
27	2.56	Luton	
28	2.48	Tower Hamlets	Inner London
29	2.44	Redbridge	Outer London
30	2.44	Forest Heath	Suffolk

Table 11: Correlations between percentages mixed by administrative area

	Mixed: white/ black Caribbean	Mixed: white/ black African	Mixed: white/ Asian	Mixed: Other
Mixed: white/black Caribbean	*	.715	.673	.709
Mixed: white/black African	.715	*	.786	.927
Mixed: white/Asian	.673	.786	*	.910
Mixed: Other	.709	.927	.910	*

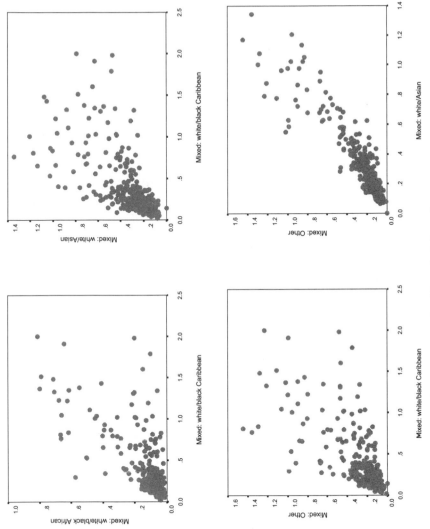

Figure 4: Scatterplots of percentage mixed by administrative areas

very high correlations between the percentage in each mixed group across areas. However, even these correlations hide the extent of the concentration. This is better shown by the scatterplots in Figure 4. These show the distribution of areas on two of the mixed percentages at a time. Not all possible pairs are shown, but these four give a good representation.

Conclusion

In conclusion what is clear is that on any measure, there are a large number of areas with very low percentages of the mixed population and a few with high percentages. These high percentages do not always go together, but there is a distinct tendency for areas high on one mixed percentage also to be higher than average on the others. Do the large numbers of mixed children mean that society is inexorably moving towards a position where more and more of the population will be mixed? Only time will tell.

Data from the Labour Force Survey, the 1991 Census and the 2001 Census are Crown Copyright and are used with permission.

References

Aspinall, P.J. (1996) *The Development of an Ethnic Question for the 2001 Census: The Findings of a Consultation Exercise of the 2001 Census Working Subgroup on the Ethnic Group Question.* London: Office for National Statistics.

Bulmer, M. (1996) The Ethnic Group Question in the 1991 Census of Population, in Coleman, D. and Salt, J. (Eds.) *Ethnicity in the 1991 Census. Volume 1: Demographic Characteristics of the Ethnic Minority Populations.* London: HMSO.

OPCS/GRO(S) (1993) *1991 Census: Ethnic Group and Country of Birth.* Great Britain. London: HMSO.

Owen, C. (2001) Mixed Race in Official Statistics, in Parker, D. and Song, M. (Eds.) *Rethinking Mixed Race.* London: Pluto Press.

Owen, D. (1996) Black-Other: The Melting Pot, in Peach, C. (Ed.) *Ethnicity in the 1991 Census, Volume 2: The Ethnic Minority Populations of Great Britain.* London: HMSO.

Phoenix, A., and Owen, C. (1996) From Miscegenation to Hybridity: Mixed Relationships and Mixed Parentage in Profile, in Bernstein, B. and Brannen, J. (Eds.) *Children, Research and Policy.* London: Taylor and Francis.

Sillitoe, K. (1978) *Ethnic Origins, 3. An Experiment in the Use of a Direct Question about Ethnicity, for the Census.* (Occasional Paper 10) London: OPCS.

Sillitoe, K. (1981) *Ethnic Origins, 4. An Experiment in the Use of a Direct Question about Ethnicity, for the Census.* (Occasional Paper 24) London: OPCS.

Sillitoe, K. (1987) *Developing Questions on Ethnicity and Related Topics for the Census.* (Occasional Paper 36) London: OPCS.

Chapter 3

Mulatto, Marginal Man, Half-Caste, Mixed Race: The One Drop Rule in Professional Practice

Kwame Owusu-Bempah

This fact is of fundamental significance in comprehending the general character-istics of the American 'mixed blood'…He is not the dejected, spiritless out-cast, neither is he the inhibited conformist. He is more likely to be restless and race conscious…radical, ambitious and creative. The lower status to which he is assigned naturally creates disconnected and rebellious feelings. From an earlier spontaneous identification with the white man, he has, under the rebuffs of a cate-gorical race prejudice, turned about and identified with the Negro race. In the process of so doing, he suffers a profound inner conflict. After all, does not the blood of white man flow through his veins? Is he not legally and morally an American citizen? And yet, he finds himself condemned to the lower caste in the American system! So the mulatto is likely to think of himself. Living in two social worlds, between which there is antagonism and prejudice, he experiences in himself the conflict.

(Stonequist, 1937: 24–25).

Introduction

As lately as 1993, Barbara Tizard and Ann Phoenix titled their book on the experiences of young persons of 'mixed race' parentage in contemporary Britain with the question: *Black, White or Mixed Race?* Although contemporarily apposite, the true significance of this question lies in the history of black and white relations, particularly in the manner in which black and white sexual liaisons have been historically perceived and their offspring treated by racist society. Such historical exploration must begin with North American anti-miscegenation laws. These written laws not only barred interracial sex and marriage, but also defined racial identity and reinforced and enforced racial hierarchy. For black people (i.e., people of African descent) the laws explicitly identified them as diminished persons under the curse of slavery and inferi-ority (Moran, 2001; Guthrie, 1976). As a further deterrent against interracial sex and its consequent offspring, in 1705, the State of Virginia, for example, passed a law which classified as a 'mulatto' the child or grandchild of a 'Negro'. Consequently, Virginia officials decreed that mulattoes must be made black, and the bondage of 'blacks' be defined and made universal (Moran, 2001). This led to the universal adoption of the 'one-drop rule'. To aid their identification and classification by officials, this rule defined as black anyone with traceable African ancestry. A further complex set of racial classification, based on (superficial) anatomical features, soon followed creating the following categories of the offspring of 'mixed bloods':

> Sambo – a person of seven-eighths (87.5 per cent) 'black blood' and one-eighths (12.5 per cent) 'white blood';
> Mango – a person who was three-quarters (75 per cent) black and one-quarter (25 per cent) white;
> Meamelouc – a person who was one-sixteenth (6.25 per cent) black and 93.75 per cent white;
> Sang-mele – a person who was one sixty-fourth (1.56 per cent) black and sixty-three sixty-fourths (98.44 per cent) white (See e.g., Herskovits, 1934; Moran, 2001).

The aim of this was to obliterate their white side. By socio-politically scraping out their white heritage, the racial classification scheme converted them into black; it turned them into individuals who, as though, had been generated by a single biological parent, as if they had been cloned. The purpose of this was to formally disenfranchise them; it precluded them from gaining official recognition of their white ancestry, thereby denying them inheritance and privileges based on their white origins. Under a 1661 Maryland anti-miscegenation law, for example, 'freeborne English women' who married 'Negro slaves' and their children were made slaves to their husbands' masters during their husbands' lifetimes (Moran, 2001). Furthermore, it identified and classified the children as mulattoes' (i.e., young mules). Elsewhere in the Western World, and at other times, they were variously referred to as 'metis' (French for a mongrel dog), 'mixed-breed', 'half-breed', 'half-caste', and so forth. In Britain, such terms as 'tinted' and 'half-caste' are still in currency amongst 'politically incorrect' groups and individuals. The above classification was blatantly lacking in biological or scientific precision. Attempts to remedy this led to a ludicrous revision of categories or degrees of 'Africaness' – African ancestry – (as opposed to 'Europeaness'): mulatto; quadroon – a person of a quarter African blood; and octoroon – a person of one-eighth African blood and seven-eighths white European.

The mulatto hypothesis and the marginal man

The likely confusion that these classifications and re-classifications might have engendered in these individuals, especially those who were classified as one-sixteenth black and those classified as one-sixty-fourth black, as 'only' 93.75% and 98.44% white respectively, prompted scholars in the late 1920s and throughout the 1930s, notably Park (1928, 1931) and Stonequist (1937) to coin the term 'marginal man' to symbolise their experiences, thus, changing the terminology within the academic community. Both Park and Stonequist defined the marginal man as a person who did not fall 'neatly' into black or white groupings in the USA at the time. As the quotation at the beginning of this discussion indicates, marginal persons naturally belonged to both black and white communities, but, often, neither was prepared to accept them. Marginal status was, therefore, seen as characterised by confusion and a myriad of problems. Culturally and socially, marginal persons were said to live in limbo. Psychologically, they were believed to experience torment, to experience psychiatric and emotional problems, low self-esteem and identity-confusion. To the point, they were claimed to be deficient in every human domain.

Hall (1992) is at pains to remind us that Stonequist's view of marginality was challenged by other sociologists and psychologists (e.g., Goldberg, 1941; Green, 1947; Wright and Wright, 1972). The most prominent complaint, in Hall's view, was that Stonequist made no distinction among marginal persons, marginal status, and marginal personality: a marginal person is biologically or culturally from two or more 'races' or cultures; whereas marginal status exists when an individual occupies a position somewhere between cultures, but does not wholly belong to any; one has a marginal personality when one has trouble dealing with the marginal status position, is torn between cultures, and develops psychological problems. These distinctions suggest that the mere fact of being a marginal person does not automatically or necessarily lead to a marginal personality. On the contrary, some believe that marginal people are multiethnic/cultural, endowed with the ability to identify with more than one culture and acquire both emic and etic perspectives and a wide range of competencies and sensitivities. Park (1937) recognised this:

> *The fate which condemns him [the marginal person] to live, the same time, in two worlds is the same which compels him to assume, in relation to the world in which he lives, the role of a cosmopolitan and a stranger. Inevitably he becomes, relative to his cultural milieu, the individual with a wider horizon, the keener intelligence, the more detached and rational viewpoint. The marginal person is always relatively the more civilised human being.*

(Hall, 1992: 251).

Despite this, there have, historically, been two diametrically opposing positions on this matter, the so-called mulatto hypothesis. Briefly, the first of these holds that race-crossing is pernicious in its effects; the second maintains that inbreeding is not conducive to survival, since new strains must be introduced into a population if fertile, virile offspring are to be assured. Absurd claims were made by those who held that race-crossing was undesirable. For example, according to Herskovits, they claimed to have found among 'Negro-white crosses in Jamaica that some of these crosses possessed the long legs of the Negro and the short arms of the white, thus putting them at a disadvantage in picking up objects from the ground' (Herskovits, 1934: 391). Like all racial myths, this myth dies hard. We still find such claims, although transmogrified, in such areas as sports, notably boxing, football and athletics (Cashmore, 1982). Gates (1929), a champion of the first hypothesis and supporter of eugenics, unequivocally summarised his position regarding black-white sexual liaisons:

> *As regards world eugenics, then, it would appear that intermixture of unrelated races, from every point of view, is undesirable, at least as regards race combinations involving one primitive and one advanced...It is, therefore, clear that miscegenation between...the white races and African races...is wholly undesirable from a eugenic or any other reasonable point of view.*
>
> (In Herskovits, 1934: 390).

Jennings (1930), a proponent of the second position, countered this assertion:

> *The Negro and the white man each have 24 pairs of chromosome. These work perfectly together, both in forming vigorous offspring, and in the much more delicate test of later uniting to form germ cells in these offspring. The same is true of crosses between any of the other races of man...*
>
> (In Herskovits, 1934: 391).

Stonequist (1937) reinforced Jennings' rebuttal when he declared, from a sociological perspective, that there are no biological problems with race mixture, only societal problems, which can account for whatever 'inferiority' of race-crossing might exhibit. Lamentably, modern writers largely seem to ignore such rebuttals and supporting evidence (Owusu-Bempah, 1997; Owusu-Bempah and Howitt, 1999). In other words, they continue to hold fast to, and perpetuate, the first 'mulatto' hypothesis which holds that people of racially 'mixed' ancestry are inferior to others. Kurt Lewin's (1935, 1941), idea of self-hatred and Kenneth and Maine Clark's (1939, 1947) studies on black children's racial mis-identification served to buttress this myth by giving it an aura of reality, an enduring quality. This canard endures in spite of the long history of research indicating the contrary (e.g., Baldwin, 1979; Beckham, 1929, 1934; Cross, 1991; Owusu-Bempah, 1994; Owusu-Bempah and Howitt, 1999, 2000a; Rosenberg, 1989; Tizard and Phoenix, 1993; Wilson, 1987).

Societal legacy

By the end of the nineteenth century, with pseudo-scientific Social Darwinism, 'race' had become firmly entrenched in Western thought, so much so that during much of the last century, most, including a significant number of intellectuals, accepted racial classification as valid biological groups akin to the species (Banton, 1987). This view, shared by many early twentieth century social scientists, circumscribed the fundamental capacities, such as intelligence of the members of the different 'races' (Kamin, 1974). It was not until around the mid-twentieth century that there began a shift in both the scientific and popular understandings of 'race'. The prevailing view today is that 'race' is a socio-political invention (Banton, 1987; Montague, 1974/1997; Howitt and Owusu-Bempah, 1994; Owusu-Bempah and Howitt, 2000a). Yet, the recognition that 'race', as applied to humankind, is a fallacy has not resulted in the abandonment of social boundaries separating not only major racial/ethnic groups, but also hues of 'white'. Anyone whose skin colour does not somehow meet the 'brilliant white' standard is viewed with suspicion: 'Where do you come from?' is very often the first question they are asked by strangers (and even familiar people). Thus, Nakashima (1992) argues that the horror of the Holocaust, with its Nazi biological determinism, only shifted the scholarly argument against interracial sex and 'mixed race' people, for example, from a biological one to an argument based on socialisation and cultural reasoning.

Children of black and white ancestry are still described by many as being unable to deal with their dual biological and cultural heritage, that they are torn between conflicting cultures, and so are confused; that their rejection by either or any 'racial' group means that they are marginal, wretched and outcast, left to be the targets of both their parent groups' anger and hatred for one another, the ridicule of others and the pity and charity of childcare professionals (Owusu-Bempah, 1994, 1997). In short, there has been very little change, either since World War II or since 1967 when the last anti-miscegenation law in the USA was repealed, in societal attitudes towards black-white sexual intimacy and the offspring of these unions. Thus many writers (e.g., Nakashima, 1992; Owusu-Bempah, 1997; Williams, 1980) agree that, in actuality, there is very little real difference between the cultural and biological arguments against miscegenation and 'mixed race' persons, in that both connote a hierarchy, with the Caucasian race and Western Anglo-Saxon culture placed above all other 'races' and cultures.

Many attribute the enduring influence of slavery and the ensuing North American anti-miscegenation laws on Western thought and society at large to an irrational fear of contamination of, a blot on, the 'pure white race' and its 'civilised' culture. For example, Walvin (1973), describing British antipathy towards interracial sexual intimacy, commented:

> ...there can be no doubt...that, by a substantial and influential section of English society, miscegenation was regarded as a threat to the structure of that society.
> (In Wilson, 1987: 2).

Stonequist (1937) had earlier made this observation when he pointed out the unwillingness of white society to distinguish between the so-called 'mixed blood' (mulattoes) and 'full blood' (Negroes). Fryer (1984) and Williams (1974) propose that 'contamination' of the white 'race' posed the greatest threat when interracial sexual relationships were voluntary, as opposed to when they occurred in the context of slavery. In modern Britain, for example, Fryer argues that many of the riots in the 1950s and 1960s against black people in Notting Hill, Nottingham, Tyneside,

Liverpool and Cardiff were a clear manifestation of this fear; they were motivated by white people's neurosis concerning any contact between black men and white women.

In another era, and in a different context, this fear was articulated in a different language. For example, in a 1941 article, leading sociologist Robert Merton is reported to have hypothesised that interracial marriage should be rare and would occur only when one partner exchanged class status for racial status, or vice-versa. On the few occasions when individuals of equal status married without any apparent benefit to their class or racial position, Merton characterised them as pariahs, or anti-social: they were either rebelling against social norms or succumbing to lusty impulses. When presented with an instance in which a white woman married down in terms of both 'race' and class, Merton saw her choice as irrational, and unaffectedly attributed it to lust:

> *[This case] is consistent with our interpretation that the upper class white woman in a union of this sort...believed that her ('Negro') husband is 'the only man who can satisfy her sexually'.*
>
> (Merton, in Moran, 2001: 113).

By marrying a black man, this woman automatically forfeited her status; she was relegated to the husband's 'Negro' status, with all its accompanying disadvantages and loss of privileges; so were her children. This is still the case in Western society, and applies regardless of which parent is black or their socio-economic status. Anne Wilson (1987) points out that British children of mixed race, Anglo-African/Caribbean parentage, are recognised as such; however this category is subsumed under the large rubric of black or African. That is, they are primarily considered and categorised as though they were 'monoracial' persons of African descent. Namely, in today's British society, white women who enter sexual relationships with black men are very often ostracised, and their children looked down on, by both their families and society at large. Alibhai-Brown and Montague (1992) in their book on interracial relationships, provide the following example, an account of a single white mother:

> *Nobody respects or understands how people like me feel. There were some skinheads the other day – scum you know – and one of them kicked my little boy, Matthew, and when I screamed they just laughed and said, 'Look, one white and three bloody wogs'.*
>
> (Alibhai-Brown and Montague, 1992: 221–23).

Throughout history, the offspring of black-white unions have usually been disparaged not only on ideological grounds, but also (pseudo) scientific ones (Guthrie, 1976). In Western society (as well as other societies, such as South Asian and East Asian societies), 'race' or caste is still seen as an unbridgeable divide, such that black people are not accepted in the same way as other 'racial' or ethnic groups are. In a racially divided world, sex and marriage between a black person and a white person are automatically pathological, indelibly fouled with irrational fears and bigotry. To an extent, the black community has been infected with this disease. Black individuals' romantic attraction to white people is oftentimes perceived disapprovingly; it is often seen as a form of self-hatred, a betrayal of black identity/culture and an acceptance of white skin as the romantic ideal, rather than being motivated by love.

Professional thinking and practice: what has changed?

Historically, social work has been influenced by race theories, beliefs and assumptions. These, in turn, have generally biased and distorted social workers' perceptions, assessments and treatment of black service-users and their needs (Owusu-Bempah, 1997: 50).

So, apart from being 'free persons' (as opposed to slaves), apart from being referred to or classified as 'biracial', 'mixed race' or 'dual heritage' (as opposed to 'sambos', 'mulattoes', 'half-caste' and so forth), what has changed in the ways in which modern racist society perceives and treats the offspring of black and white intimate unions, especially those who come into contact with statutory childcare agencies and professionals? Research suggests that very little has changed. They still face hostility and disdain in important sectors of society: education, health and social care and employment. Today, the offspring of black and white unions still continue to be subject to pathologising by both black and white professionals – social workers, teachers, and therapists. Practitioners hang on to the myth that personality and other psychological problems plague these children and young people. The following section presents two recent studies, involving social work trainees, to illustrate the point.

The research

Placed in historical context, it becomes patent why the patterns of childcare practitioners' treatment of children of 'mixed race' parentage is remarkably consistent between Britain and the USA. In the public childcare system, for example, research has repeatedly found that, compared to white children, African-American children and children of 'mixed race' parentage in the USA are not only over-represented, but also do stay longer in care, are moved about to more foster families, and less likely to be adopted (e.g., Barth, 1997; Courtney et al., 1996). Research carried out in the UK over the past 30 years reveals disturbing similarities (Batta and Mawby, 1981; Foren and Batta, 1970; Katz, 1996). One early study (Batta et al., 1975) found that children of 'mixed race' parentage were at least eight times more likely to be admitted into care than white or African-Caribbean or Asian children. Follow-up studies, six years later, confirmed previous findings that these children entered care more often, that their average age of entry was younger, and they spent longer periods in care (Batta and

Mawby, 1981). In recent years, Barn (1990, 1993, 1999; Barn et al., 1997) has carried out a series of investigations and reviews of studies of children entering UK local authority care. These studies and reviews indicate that children of 'mixed race' parentage continue to be disadvantaged in the system, to be disproportionately over-represented, and are more likely to be admitted into local authority care than other children are. In one of their reviews, Barn et al. (1997) concluded:

> *While African Caribbean and Asian families are considered suitable for children of African Caribbean and Asian backgrounds [respectively], children of mixed parentage presented a dilemma for social workers.*
>
> (Barn et al., 1997: 281).

Given the foregoing discussion, it is not so difficult to see why these children represent a challenge to social workers and other childcare professionals. Historically, the 'one-drop' rule decreed that they be seen and treated as black. Today, duplicitous, 'political correctness' mandates that they be seen as something else (Owusu-Bempah, 2003) yet, no one has clearly defined what their ethnic category is, or how they ought to be treated. Thus, in situations of uncertainty or ambiguity, practitioners are prone to resort to myths, stereotypes, assumptions and prejudices concerning these children. In social work, as in education and healthcare, the mulatto hypothesis and the marginal man notion provide prêt-à-porter stereotypes and assumptions (Owusu-Bempah, 1994). To remind readers, the former holds that 'mixed-blood' individuals are inferior to others, while the latter portrays them as culturally, socially and psycho-logically wretched. Evidence regarding the influence of these myths on contemporary childcare practice in the UK abounds. In health care, for example, Dummett (1984) reported a health visitor's curt summary of her perceived causes of the problems facing children of 'mixed race' parentage: 'The problem lies in the mixtures' (Dummett, 1984: 177). As recently as 1998, Connolly reported similar views expressed by a primary school teacher about a child whose father was in prison at the time of the study. These included also banal stereotypes and assumptions about black men, and white women in interracial sexual relationships:

> *One day I had a to-do with him [Paul] and, because he doesn't even, he tends to be a bit wild; he doesn't listen to what you are saying...But I shall imagine Paul's father is **a big West Indian man**, because Paul is quite big and the **mother is blonde...***
>
> (Connolly, 1998: 94) (Emphasis added).

In social work theory, policy and practice, the influence of both the mulatto hypothesis and the idea of the 'marginal man' is almost addictive. This is most evident in the fostering and adoption arena (Owusu-Bempah, 1997, 2002). Coward and Dattani (1993) provide a case in point. They draw attention to how, in the case of children and adolescents of 'mixed race' parentage, child protection case conferences and statutory childcare reviews routinely, and virtually automatically, result in requests for professional intervention to deal with their psychological problems which are seen as resulting from their culture- and identity-confusion. Mullender (1991) also emphasised the 'benefits' of a project designed specifically to improve the self-confidence of those children who ostensibly felt confused about their racial identity as a consequence of being adopted or fostered by white families. These assessments ignore obvious alternative explanatory factors, for example separation and loss (Owusu-Bempah, 1995; Owusu-Bempah and Howitt, 1997, 2000b). Other Systematic activities to deal with these youngsters' putative psychological disturbance involve, explicitly or implicitly, denying their white heritage (e.g. Banks, 1992; Maxime, 1991, 1993a). Practitioners seem oblivious to evidence suggesting the undesirability of this practice, its exacting psychological and emotional anguish it causes these youngsters (Owusu-Bempah and Howitt, 1999; Tizard and Phoenix, 1993). Many casually accept this practice. Worse still, others go further and recommend it as a necessary anti-racist strategy for social work with these children (e.g. Small, 1991; Thompson, 1993). The work of clinicians involved with these children (e.g., Banks, 1992; Coleman, 1994; McRoy and Freeman, 1986) also suggest that social services departments and educational establishments still believe in the mulatto hypothesis and the 'marginal man' (albeit subconsciously) and so have established, or support, special clinics to 'repair the damaged self-identity' of black children in their care, to improve their racial identity, to cultivate a sense of being black or black pride into them. (See Owusu-Bempah, 2002 and Owusu-Bempah and Howitt, 1999 for a detailed discussion).

Race and social work trainees

The influence of race theories, beliefs and assumptions on childcare practice with children of 'mixed race' parentage refuses to abate. The following two recent empirical studies, conducted independently and a few years apart, support this view. They demonstrate the enduring and pervasive influence of race among even to-day's social work trainees.

Study 1

Stephen's best friends are white, so may be confused about his identity '…awareness of being different, i.e., colour, feeling of shame about his origin'. Stephen has problems reconciling with his own identity, he may be trying to be white' (Owusu-Bempah, 1994: 132).

These were some of the comments made by social work students about a fictitious child of 'mixed race' parentage. The students participated in a study which investigated the prevalence amongst social workers of the belief in black children's negative self-concept, and also the extent of the influence of this view on children and families social work. The respondents (N=102) were post-graduate social work students at two Universities in separate regions of the midlands of England. They responded individually to three randomly distributed vignettes which were identical with the sole exception of the racial/ethnic backgrounds of the principal characters: a white boy, a boy of 'mixed race' parentage, and a black boy. The respondents' task was to assess the possible causes of the children's behaviour-problems as well as their developmental needs – their social, emotional and intellectual needs. They were also required to suggest possible courses of intervention to promote the children's well-being. (See Owusu-Bempah, 1994 for details).

The students' responses were analysed according to the frequency with which particular causes of the children's behaviour and particular course of action to meet their needs were mentioned. Causal factors mentioned ranged from identity-confusion to family circumstances, including parenting. Analysis of the results revealed racial differences in the respondents' attributions and recommendations. In the first place, 85% of those who responded to the vignette involving the child of 'mixed race' parentage attributed his difficulties to identity-crisis, and 59% and only 25% of those who responded to the vignettes involving the black child and the white child respectively mentioned identity-crisis as a causal factor in the children's difficulties. The respondents' recommended intervention programmes were equally telling: identity-work was the commonest recommended intervention for the child of 'mixed race parentage (55%); to an extent, this was also true for the black child (35%), whereas identity-work was hardly recommended for the white child (9%); the provision of information about cultural heritage was virtually not mentioned in the case of the white boy (3%), but was recommended for the boy of 'mixed race' parentage (39%) and the black boy (19%). These findings support Coward and Datanni's (1993) earlier observation. These attributions and recommendations ignored the core-cause of the children's difficulties, especially in the case of the child of 'mixed race' parentage. In other words, the social work trainees' assessments and recommendations were not based upon objective facts; instead, they were heavily influenced by centuries-old racial myths, and consequently recommended psychologically potentially noxious intervention programmes, particularly for the child of 'mixed race' parentage.

Kirton (1999), conducted an attitude survey of 835 social work students on race and adoption. The study focused on attitudes towards trans-racial and same-race adoption and fostering. The three main findings of interest to the present discussion were:

1. Support for same-race placement (ethnic matching) was more noticeable among black students than among their white counterparts.
2. The notion of 'black identity' was found to be the most influential factor in the students' views on race and adoption/fostering.
3. There was resistance to labelling children of 'mixed race' parentage as black.

Kirton reported also that the issues which generated the strongest disagreement amongst the students were those concerning white families' capacity to cater for the identity and cultural needs of black children, and also the need to personally experience racism in order to help a child cope with it.

Many writers have effectively countered these claims (e.g., Owusu-Bempah, 1989; 1997; Owusu-Bempah and Howitt, 1999; Tizard and Phoenix, 1989, 1993; Wilson, 1987). However, Kirton discusses the implications of this study's findings in terms of current debate regarding policy and practice in the family placement of children of 'mixed race' parentage. Out of historical context, this debate is less than meaningful; it requires awareness and understanding of anti-miscegenation laws (written and unwritten) and their consequent mulatto hypothesis and the marginal man notion to fully grasp its significance. This is particularly pertinent in view of the respondents' reluctance to identify children of 'mixed race' parentage as black or white. It reinforces the original notion of the 'marginal man' which holds that they owe their disadvan-taged status in racist society to the fact that both the white community and the black community shun them. On the other hand, Kirton's finding that black students involved in the study were more supportive of same-race placement may easily be explained in terms of 'political correctness' (Owusu-Bempah, 2003). In today's British society, political correctness compels these children to affiliate with the so-called black community, and to be accepted by it; it is claimed that their psychological salvation lies solely in identifying with the black community, in adopting 'black culture' and developing a 'black identity' (Banks, 1992; Goldstein, 1999; Maxime, 1991a, b, 1993; Small, 1991). The telling question is: In what manner is this different from the one-drop rule?

Negating their self-definition

Society and its controlling agents, including practitioners such as social workers, teachers, and mental health personnel, continue to harbour negative attitudes towards the offspring of black and white sexual unions (Owusu-Bempah, 1994; Root, 1992). Owusu-Bempah and Howitt (1999, 2000a) have argued that the popular belief that culture-confusion and its concomitant psychological and emotional problems are endemic to these children is no more than a racist assumption. It is the ghost of the 'marginal man' evoked to haunt them, to justify our unfair treatment of them. Two of the several questions we need to ask ourselves are: Do we know, are we aware of, or do we even care about the damaging effects that our racial beliefs, assumptions and stereotypes may have on our practice and, consequently, on these children? Are we aware of the damage we inflict upon their psychological functioning, as well as their life-chances, as a result of our denying them self-definition? (Owusu-Bempah, 1994, 1997). Research indicates that children of 'mixed race' parentage become hypersen-sitive to situations in which others or groups attempt to define them in ways which are inconsistent with their own self-definition (e.g., Brown, 1993; Bowles, 1993). Such evidence suggests further that this sensitivity is heightened when childcare professionals join or collude with others to pressure them to accept or confirm the social identity we impose over their self-concept; that when this happens, feelings of confusion, isolation and loss of orientation frequently result.

Typically, we do not view their efforts to claim dual membership to black and white groups as an acceptable option for them (e.g., Banks, 1992; Maxime, 1991a; Milner, 1975, 1983), despite the fact that they have a legitimate claim to both groups. We disregard the fact that exerting such pressure upon them makes them feel obliged to make a choice between black and white worlds (Hall, 1992). In other words, instead of helping them to develop their own sense of monoculturalism, multi-culturalism, or bi-'racialism', as the case may be, we strive to impose upon them the culture or membership of the group which we perceive to be 'inferior', usually 'black culture' or group (Montague, 1974;1997; Owusu-Bempah and Howitt, 1999). Placing them in this position is not just unnecessary, but, more importantly, damaging, as much research has indicated (e.g., Brown, 1993; Owusu-Bempah, 1997, 2002; Tizard and Phoenix, 1993).

The title of an article (Goldstein, 1999), outwardly championing the interest and welfare of children of 'mixed race' parentage, reveals the continuing marginalisation of these children. As the title indicates, it focuses on 'black children with a white parent' in Britain. The paper describes the psycho-political process of their identity-development, and advocates that a viable means by which they can normalise is to identify themselves as 'black with a white parent'. It claims that this will enable them to reject the forces that pathologise them. From what the author claims to be a 'post-modernist black perspective', it concludes:

> ...the 'racial' self-concepts that are available to this group, identifying their under-lying agendas and their consequences...the availability of the self-concept 'black with a white parent', offered in the framework of change, multiplicity and individuality, is beneficial.

(Goldstein, 1999: 285).

Whatever this assertion may mean, one thing is clear: it is question-begging. Yet, it raises several revealing questions. For example: To whom is the self-concept, 'black with a white parent', beneficial, the children or proponents of the one-drop rule? Alternatively, why can they not identify themselves as 'white with a black parent', and why will this self-concept not be equally beneficial? In short, is this not, yet another euphemism (hypocritical political correctness) for 'sambo', 'mulatto', etc., a surreptitious attempt to continue to deny these children self-definition, something most of us take for granted?

Effects on the children

Stonequist (1937) was among the first to describe the marginal personality as a broad composite of possible features. That is, not every individual in marginal circumstances necessarily experiences the characteristics associated with marginality. The degree and intensity of marginal experiences depends upon both the person's indigenous characteristics, such as temperament, intelligence; also their situational factors will affect the intensity of the marginal experience. He noted also that the social position of 'mixed blood' persons is inextricably intertwined with the larger issue of racism; that the complex web of individual, institutional and cultural racism perpetuates the distinct status differentials for those who are not white in a white society without being accorded full membership in any group. Like Montague (1997), Brown (1990) concurs:

The core traits which characterize the biracial person arise from the nature of inter-group relations, not the specific cultural content within particular groups. Each group, especially the one in power, seeks to protect itself by keeping the other in its place and maintaining social distance. The significance of ethnic differences and characteristics is thus a matter of social definition.

(Brown, 1990: 334).

Various investigators in Britain and the USA report that most, if not all, young adult children from black and white sexual liaisons are confused and feel uncomfortable identifying with one side of the parental line against the other. These young adults experience feelings of disloyalty arising from being forced to disown 50% of who they are. Feelings of shame and anxiety are also evident in these young adult children (e.g., Bowles, 1993; Tizard and Phoenix, 1993). Thus, Connolly (1998) argues that to expect children of black and white unions to behave like a black person or white person is unrealistic; that in view of their unique developmental history, their dual inheritance, it would be more appropriate to assess them psychologically on the basis of their dual frames of reference rather than trying to stereotype or mis-categorise them.

This suggests that if a child dis-identifies with or disowns a parent, they cannot use that parent as a reflective object presenting to the child who they are. If reflection is not possible, the child is likely to experience difficulties in developing and differentiating their 'real' self. The child may, therefore, feel a sense of emptiness, abandonment and alienation as a consequence of disowning a substantial part (at least 50%) of their genealogy. On the other hand, if the child is encouraged to incorporate both sides of themselves, they are able to develop a sense of connectedness, psychological wholeness (Owusu-Bempah, 1995; Owusu-Bempah and Howitt, 1997, 2000b). For example, Blatt and Wild (1976) reported that young adults described feeling great pleasure in seeing themselves reflected in relatives and in being told that they resembled someone from an earlier generation. Thus, they suggested that the discovery of important others precedes the discovery of oneself. The present author's research on socio-genealogical connectedness suggests that this is equally applicable to children of 'mixed race' parentage. Briefly, the inability to own both sides of one's biological and/or cultural heritage impedes the construction of a solid sense of self. Bowles (1993) stresses that acceptance of one part at the expense of the other part is not a psychological option, despite its political correctness. That is, failure to identify with one parent robs the child of identification with that parent, so that the parent cannot be integrated into one's self-concept, leading to feelings of shame, guilt, emotional isolation and depression. The authors believe that while these issues have, up until now, been mandated that the offspring of black and white unions be viewed as black, this stance has not taken note of the psychological meaning of disowning a part of oneself. They ardently advise us to discard this view, so that we may re-visit and re-examine the process of these children's identity-development, self-perception, and ultimately their psychological functioning.

Conclusion

A close examination of the literature suggests that marginal persons are those whose socialisation has ill-prepared them to play the role assigned them in the social sphere. This is simply because there are forces preventing them from making their reference group a membership group. In other words, marginal status is created by the society and structures and rules that order it, and benefit from them. Otherwise, what explanation can we adduce for Tizard and Phoenix's (1993) finding that the majority, if not all, of 'mixed race' children in contemporary Britain see themselves as English, Scottish, Welsh or simply British, and yet we insist that they are 'foreigners', that their white genetic and cultural heritage is alien to them. Is it not because, as Montague (1997), and Root (1992), have argued, they represent living and growing evidence that the proscriptions and prescriptions governing interracial relations, especially sexual relations, have been violated? Root's straightforward answer is in the affirmative:

> *The presence of racially mixed persons defies the social order predicated upon race, blurs racial and ethnic group boundaries, and challenges generally accepted proscriptions and prescriptions regarding intergroup relations. Furthermore, and perhaps most threatening, the existence of racially mixed persons challenges long-held notions about the biological, moral, and social meaning of race.*

(Root, 1992: 3)

Do we, as twenty-first century child-welfare professionals, want to keep alive the biological, moral and social meaning of 'race'? Do we want to continue to police the taboo surrounding black and white sexual intimacy on the behalf of racist society? In short, do we want to continue to practice and perpetuate the one-drop rule in our work with children of 'mixed race' parentage? Rather, it is incumbent upon us not to just disdain or refrain from this pernicious, fallacious notion. We must accept it as our duty to counteract it not only in our practice, but also in society at large. Simply, to provide a professional service to children of 'mixed race' parentage, attitudes must change; we must discard our racial myths and beliefs, our racial stereotypes and assumptions about the offspring of interracial sexual intimacy.

References

Alibhai-Brown, Y. and Montague, A. (1992) *The Colour of Love: Mixed Race Relationships*. London: Virago.

Baldwin, J.A. (1979) Theory and Research Concerning the Notion of Black Self-hatred: A Review and Reinterpretation. *Journal of Black Psychology*, 5: 51–77.

Banks, N. (1992) Some Considerations of 'Racial' Identity and Self-esteem when Working with Mixed Ethnicity and Their Mothers as Social Services Clients. *Social Services Review*, 3: 32–41.

Banton, M. (1987) *Racial Theories*. Cambridge: Cambridge University Press.

Barn, N. (1990) Black Children in Local Authority Care: Admission Patterns. *New Community*, 16: 2.

Barn, R. (1993) *Black Children in the Public Care System*. London: Batsford.

Barn, R. (1999) White Mothers, Mixed-Parentage Children and Child Welfare. *British Journal of Social Work*, 29: 269–84.

Barn, R., Sinclair, R. and Ferdinand, D. (1997) *Acting on Principle: An Examination of Race and Ethnicity in Social Services Provision for Children and Families*. London: BAAF.

Barth, R.P. (1997) Effects of Age and Race on the Odds of Adoption Versus Remaining in Long-term Out-of-home Care. *Child Welfare*, 27: 285–308.

Batta, I. and Mawby, R. (1981) Children in Local Authority Care: A Monitoring of Racial Differences in Bradford. *Policy and Politics*, 9: 2, 137–49.

Beckham, A.S. (1929) A Study of Race Attitudes in Negro Children and of Adolescent Age. *Journal of Abnormal and Social Psychology*, 39: 18–29.

Beckham, A.S. (1934) Is the Negro Happy? A Psychological Analysis. *Journal of Abnormal and Social Psychology*, 24: 186–90.

Blatt, S.J. and Wild, C.M. (1976) *Schizophrenia: A Developmental Approach*. New York: Academic Press.

Bowles, D.D. (1993) BiRacial Identity: Children Born to African-American and White Couples. *Clinical Social Work Journal*, 21: 417–27.

Brown, P.M. (1990) Biracial Identity and Social Marginality. *Child and Adolescent Social Work*, 7: 319–37.

Cashmore, E.E. (1982) *Black Sportsmen*. London: Routledge.

Clark, K. B. and Clark, M. (1939) The Development of the Consciousness of Self and Emergence of Racial Identity in Negro Pre-School Children. *Journal of Social Psychology* 10: 591–99.

Clark, K. B. and Clark, M. (1947) Racial Identification and Preference in Negro Children, in Newcombe, T. M. and Hartley, E. L. (Eds) *Readings in Social Psychology*. New York. Rinehart Winston. 602–11.

Coleman, J. (1994) Black Children in Care: Crisis of Identity. *The Runnymede Trust Bulletin*, October, 4.

Connolly, P. (1998) *Racism, Gender Identities and Young Children: Social Relations in a Multi-Ethnic, Inner-City Primary School.* London: Routledge.

Courtney, M., Barth, R.P., Berrick, J.D., Brooks, D., Needel, D. and Park, L. (1996) Race and Child Welfare Services: Past Research and Future Directions. *Child Welfare,* 75: 99–137.

Coward, B. and Dattani, P. (1993) Race, Identity and Culture, in Dwivedi. K.N. (Ed.) *Group Work with Children and Adolescents: A Handbook.* London: Jessica Kingsley.

Cross, W.E. (1991) *Shades of Black: Diversity in African–American Identity.* Philadelphia. Temple University Press.

Dummett, A. (1984) *A Portrait of English Racism.* London, Pluto.

Fryer, P. (1984) *Staying Power.* London, Pluto.

Foren, R. and Batta, I. (1970) 'Colour' as a Variable in the Use Made of a Local Authority Child Care Department'. *Social Work,* 27: 3, 10–5.

Gates, R.R. (1929) Heredity in Man, in Herskovits, M.J. (1934) A Critical Discussion of the 'Mulatto Hypothesis'. *Journal of Negro Education.* 389.

Goldberg, M.M. (1941) Qualification of the Marginal Man Theory. *American Sociological Review,* 6: 52–8.

Goldstein, B.P. (1999) Black, with a White Parent, a Positive and Achievable Identity. *British Journal of Social Work,* 29: 285–301.

Green, A.W. (1947) A Re-examination of the Marginal Man Concept. *Social Forces,* 26: 167–71.

Guthrie, R. (1976) *Even the Rat was White: A Historical View of Psychology.* New York: Harper and Row.

Hall, C. (1997) Cultural Malpractice: The Growing Obsolescence of Psychology with the Changing US Population. *American Psychologist,* 52: 642–51.

Hall, C.C.I. (1992) Please Choose One: Ethnic Identity Choices for Biracial Individuals, in Root, M.P.P. (Ed.) *Racially Mixed People in America.* London: Sage.

Herskovits, M.J. (1934) A Critical Discussion of the 'Mulatto Hypothesis'. *Journal of Negro Education,* 389–402.

Howitt, D. and Owusu-Bempah, J. (1994) *The Racism of Psychology: Time for Change.* Hemel Hempstead: Harvester Wheatsheaf.

Jennings, H.S. (1930) The Biological Basis of Human Nature, in Herskovits, M.J. (1934) A Critical Discussion of the Mulatto Hypothesis. *Journal of Negro Education,* 390.

Kamin, L.J. (1974) *The Science and Politics of IQ.* New York: Wiley.

Katz, I. (1996) *The Construction of Racial Identity in Children of Mixed Parentage: Mixed Metaphors.* London: Jessica Kingsley.

Kirton, D. (1999) Perspectives on 'Race' and Adoption: The Views of Student Social Workers. *British Journal of Social Work,* 29: 779–96.

Lewin, K. (1935) Psycho-sociological Problems of a Minority Group. *Character and Personality,* 3: 175–87.

Lewin, K. (1941) Jewish Self-hatred. *Contemporary Jewish Record,* 4: 219–32.

Maxime, J.E. (1991a) Some Psychological Models of Black Self-concept, in Ahmed, S.J., Cheetham, J. and Small, J. (Eds.) *Social Work with Black Children and their Families.* London: Batsford.

Maxime, J.E. (1991b) *Black like Me Workbook One: Black Identity.* Beckenham: Emani Publications.

Maxime, J.E. (1993) The Importance of Racial Identity for the Psychological Well-being of Black Children. *Association of Child Psychology and Psychiatry Review and Newsletter,* 15: 4, 173–9.

McRoy, R.G. and Freeman, E. (1986) Racial Identity Issues Among Mixed Race Children. *Social Work Education* 8: 164–74.

Milner, D. (1983) *Children and Race: Ten Years On.* London: Ward Lock Educational.

Milner, D. (1975) *Children and Race.* Harmondsworth: Penguin.

Montague, A. (1974) *Mans' Most Dangerous Myth: The Fallacy of Race.* New York: Oxford University Press.

Montague, A. (1997) *Man's Most Dangerous Myth: The Fallacy of Race.* 6th edn. Walnut Creek: AltaMira Press.

Moran, R.F. (2001) *Interracial Intimacy: The Regulation of Race and Romance.* Chicago: Chicago University Press.

Mullender, A. (1991) The Ebony Project: Bicultural Group Work with Transracial Foster Parents. *Social Work with Groups,* 13: 34–41.

Nakashima, C.L. (1992) An Invisible Monster: The Creation and Denial of Mixed Race People in America, in Root, M.P.P. (Ed.) *Racially Mixed People in America.* London: Sage.

Owusu-Bempah, J. (1989) Does Colour Matter? *Community Care,* 26 January: 18–9.

Owusu-Bempah, J. (1994) Race, Self-identity and Social Work. *British Journal of Social Work,* 24: 123–36.

Owusu-Bempah, J. (1995) Information about the Absent Parent as an Important Factor in the Well-being of Children of Single-parent Families. *International Social Work,* 38: 253–75.

Owusu-Bempah, J. (1997). Race: A Framework for Social Work? in Davies, M. (Ed.) *The Blackwell Companion to Social Work.* Oxford: Blackwell.

Owusu-Bempah, J. (2002). Culture, Ethnicity and Identity, in Davies, M. (Ed.) *The Blackwell Companion to Social Work.* 2nd edn. Oxford: Blackwell.

Owusu-Bempah, K. and Howitt, D. (1999) Even Their Soul is Defective. *The Psychologist,* 12: 3, 126–30.

Owusu-Bempah, K. and Howitt, D. (2000a) *Psychology Beyond Western Perspectives.* Oxford: Blackwell.

Owusu-Bempah, K. and Howitt, D. (2000b). Socio-genealogical Connectedness: On the Role of Gender and Same-gender Parenting in Mitigating the Effects of Parental Divorce. *Child and Family Social Work,* 5: 107–16.

Park, R. (1928) Human Migration and the Marginal Man. *American Journal of Sociology,* 33: 881–93.

Park, R. (1931) The Mentality of Racial Hybrids. *American Journal of Sociology,* 36: 534–51.

Root, M.P.P. (1992) (Ed.) *Racially Mixed People in America.* Newbury Park: Sage.

Root, M.P.P. (1992) Within, Between and Beyond Race, in Root, M.P.P. (Ed.) *Racially Mixed People in America.* London: Sage.

Rosenburg, M. (1989) Old Myths Die Hard: The Case of Black Self-Esteem. *Revue Internationale De Psychologie Social.* 2:3. 357–65.

Small, J. (1991) Transracial Placements: Conflicts and Contradictions, in Ahmed, S., Cheetham, J. and Small, J. (Eds.) *Social Work with Black Children and their Families: Child Care Policy and Practice.* London: Batford/BAAF.

Stonequist, E. (1937) *The Marginal Man: A Study in Personality and Culture Conflict.* New York: Russell and Russell.

Thompson, N. (1993) *Anti-Discriminatory Social Work.* London: Macmillan.

Tizard, B. and Phoenix, A. (1989) Black Identity and Transracial Adoption. *New Community,* 15: 427–37.

Tizard, B. and Phoenix, A. (1993) *Black, White or Mixed Race: Race and Racism in the Lives of Young People of Mixed Parentage.* London: Routledge.

Williams, R.L. (1980) The Death of White in the Black Community, in Jones, R.L. (Ed.) *Black Psychology.* 2nd edn. New York: Harper and Row.

Williams, C. (1974) *The Destruction of Black Civilization: Great Issues of a Race From 4500 BC to 2000 AD.* Chicago: Third World Press.

Wilson, A. (1987) *Mixed Race Children: A Study of Identity.* London: Allen and Unwin.

Wright, R.D. and Wright, S.N. (1972) A Plea for a Further Refinement of the Marginal Man Theory, in Root, M.P.P. (Ed.) (1992) *Racially Mixed People in America.* London: Sage.

Chapter 4

The Social and Psychological Development of Mixed Parentage Children

Ilan Katz and Amal Treacher

Introduction

Mixing 'races' evokes strong feelings and fantasies, and these emotions and imaginations arise from views and values that centre on a 'pure' and an 'authentic' identity. Interracial families and mixed race children have long been viewed as microcosms of race relations in society as a whole (Wilson, 1987). They can be at the end of contradictory perceptions and representations. For some (Rustin, 1991; Phinney, 1996), they are the embodiment of the hopes, conflicts, desires and aspirations of the collectivity. Racial mixing represents a source of optimism and proof that different 'races' and cultures can live together. For others, however, they embody all the conflicts and complications associated with race relations and will inevitably experience difficulties and confusion – in short, they are a problem that needs sorting out. There seems to be little room to address the complexity and diversity experienced by mixed race children. In this chapter we would like to explore some of the current debates around 'mixed race (or biracial or dual heritage or mixed parentage), 'identity' and 'development', and hope to advance the debate, especially as it is formulated in the social work context. Whilst not offering solutions – the debate continuously evolves as the social context develops – we would hope to add to the move away from polarisation and duality to a more complex understanding of children's needs. We go on to question whether the debate about identity is really the fundamental issue for mixed race children, and argue for a broader understanding of their needs than the rather limited focus on personal identity that has characterised the literature.

It is important to recognise the context in which the debate about mixed race children is taking place. The situation in America, where much of the original literature emerged is very different both politically and demographically from the UK. There is also a theoretical division between a cognitive/behaviourist psychology concerned with knowing which side you are on versus a cultural theory and psychoanalytic theoretical framework concerned with understanding that you are.

Why is mixed race a problem?

Race has long been associated with 'blood' and is seen as something inherent in the genes and as part of nature. Interracial relationships and dual heritage children are perceived in this culture (British, European, American) as 'unnatural'. Social myths operate powerfully against mixed race relationships and these tend to centre on the mixing of blood – what we all know is that for a mix of blood to occur there had to be a mix of other fluids as well. The socially grounded myths are pervasive. Although they are false, they operate in such a way that they structure our relationships with one another, and our relationships to ourselves. These myths have a social message and the strong injunction is not to mix up categories, that the 'pure' blood should not be mixed with the 'tainted' blood of the *Other*. This belief, in part, arises from the 'one drop' rule and was part of the US race classification laws, and while historical it is a belief that lives on in the present.

There tends to be a more visceral response to the mixing of races as opposed to other mixings such as Catholic/Protestant, Muslim/Jew, or other religious or cultural pairings. Societies may respond negatively to inter-religious marriages – within families and communities they can be regarded with abhorrence and the couple involved excommunicated, treated as dead by one or both parents[1]. However inter-racial relationships can have a more lasting and deep-rooted effect in that the children (and grandchildren) are identifiably physically different from 'pure bloods'. It must also be acknowledged that there are other conflicted identities (e.g. gay/Christian), which are not to do with dual heritage or race that can lead to personal tragedy and confusion. These relationships are treated very differently in the professional literature and professionals tend not to load them with negative perceptions.

The dominant argument (Small, 1986; Banks, 1992; Maximé, 1993) is that because race is such an emotive and potentially damaging factor in children's lives, it is essential for mixed race children to have a positive identity to counterbalance the social effects of 'mixedness'. The mainstream theorists focus on a solid self-esteem and argue that positive self-images and role models prepare black children for a white, racist society. Mixed race people, in this account have to identify as black in order to survive, and because being black is their true identity.

Psychological well-being, self-esteem and social competence are seen as crucial to this identity. Children who are confused or worried about their identity will have low self-esteem, so mixed race children need to develop a single coherent image of themselves, and to positively identify with a single group of people. Moreover, they have to identify with the black group otherwise they will be ill-equipped to deal with racism, and the racist society that they inevitably inhabit. White parents, especially lone white mothers, are ill equipped to help them do so, and they require support and help from identity specialists who understand their children's needs and the methods required

---

[1] see Alibhai-Brown (2001), Chapter 5 for a more extended discussion of the issues involved.

for raising their self-esteem. This argument directs its critical gaze on white mothers, who are seen to be the cause of the psychological problems of their children (Prevatt-Goldstein, 1999; Holland and Holland, 1984). Black mothers are assumed to be able to instil an adequate black identity and fathers (white and black) are given the status of 'role models', somewhat distanced from the day-to-day lives of their children, and not particularly engaged in their deeper psychological development.

In contrast to the dichotomies presented by the mainstream theories the cultural theory framework focuses on the complexity of identity to argue that all identities are problematic – neither positive nor negative – but all have their challenges and promises. Moreover, identity is always in process, does not have an easy resting place and issues of identification and the unconscious intervene to complicate identity and relationships between self and other.

One of the issues that continue to haunt mixed race people is that of nomenclature. Embedded in this seemingly superficial concern is the nexus of issues that face them. To draw on mixed race draws on race as a biological, essentialist category; mixed-parentage along with mixed race indicates mixed up and confusion. This term was developed to replace a number of offensive terms used historically (mulatto, half-caste, half-breed). Dual heritage – the term currently in vogue, avoids offence, but at the expense of being vague and misleading – there are many people with dual heritage who are of the same 'race'. 'Mixed race' and 'dual heritage' share with other terms such as 'biracial', 'bicultural, 'dual parentage' the implication of a binary opposition where the reality is most often a complex intermingling. The current American terms 'Multiracial' and 'Multiethnic' are perhaps the best descriptors, but are potentially confusing because in the UK they are used to describe areas or groups rather than individuals.

The interface between race and culture is another complication. A child may be from two different 'races' but her parents may have grown up in the same community sharing the same culture, values and lifestyle. Another child may be a 'pure' black or white child, but have parents who come from very different, even conflicting cultural or political backgrounds. The classifications are also dependent on national context – in Germany, for example, the term 'race' has connotations of Nazism, and so they prefer to use the term 'bicultural', and include German/Serb and even German/Italian in the classification (Frieben-Blum et al., 2000). There is no easy designation to use – all repeat well-worn ideas and suppositions. We are using the inadequate term 'mixed race' here to indicate not only colour but culture, ethnicity, language, religion and those aspects of life that make up lived experience. We also recognise that the group of people we are talking about is not a defined category, but can change over time as demography and culture evolves.

Similarly, it is important to recognise that the social context is changing – more children are mixed race, there are more representations of mixed race people in the media and more mixed race people are in the public arena (Asthana, 2004). While there are still too few media representations of mixed race people and interracial relationships, there are examples of mixed race relationships in popular TV series such as Eastenders and ER. The sportsmen Tiger Woods, Rio Ferdinand and Jason Robinson, the singers Sade and Craig David, the politicians Paul Boating and Oonah King and the author Zaidie Smith – are all examples of prominent mixed race individuals. It has become much more commonplace, in London at least, to see mixed race couples out and about. There is also a growing literature of mixed race autobiographies (Parker and Song, 2001); and a number of websites (mainly USA based) for and about mixed race people (e.g. www.mavin.net; www.multiracial.com; www.ameasite.org). The presence indicates important shifts in the public and social imaginary. It remains unclear, however, how these changes are impacting on the experiences and identities of mixed race children and adults. It is important neither to leap into a false optimism or a nothing-has-changed position as the situation is fluid with some fundamental changes but a lot that remains stubbornly the same.

Identity

The arguments about the precarious psychological state of mixed race children draw upon the work of the 'marginal theorists' Park (1928) and Stonequist (1937). Marginal theory initially addressed the situation of groups of people on the margins of mainstream cultures – minority groups, immigrants, and mixed race people came to represent the archetypal marginal group. The fundamental premise is well put by Park who describes 'a man (sic) living and sharing in the cultural life and traditions of two distinct peoples; never quite willing to break, even if he were permitted to do so, with his past and his traditions and not quite accepted in the new society in which he now sought to find a place' (Park, 1928: 892).

This theoretical stance assumes that mixed race people are likely to be confused about their identity because they are caught between two opposing views of themselves. They are able to resolve their identity in two ways. Firstly (if their colouring is light enough) they can pass for white and deny their black heritage. Although this solution gains entry to the higher status group, it is achieved at a heavy psychological price, as they have to deny a part of themselves and lead a life of deceit. The other option is that they can identify as a part of the black minority. This is the healthier option, as mixed race people do not have to deny their origins, can identify with the minority group and minimise the sense of isolation. However, marginal theory is not optimistic about the psychological outcome for the majority of mixed race individuals as it is believed that they are destined to live a life torn between two races or cultures, and thereby are likely to be rejected by both groups.

The marginal theory is very persuasive and makes sense. It seems obvious that an individual torn between two cultures will suffer. But the terms in which it is cast – confusion, dislocation, denial, and poor self-esteem are emotive and loaded, and they need to be used with tentative care. This applies equally to terms that draw upon loaded language such as 'positive', 'authentic' and 'true identities'. The use of language is crucial so that people are not reduced to simple, flat beings and forced into crude positions. Cohen (1994), argues that:

> ...those who have asserted that 'race' makes a whole world of difference to the making of identity and those who argue that it should be irrelevant have tended to assume that to have a satisfactory identity is to possess a unitary sense of self in which nothing is lacking.

> (Cohen, 1994: 70)

Projections can circulate every-which-way into mixed race people, who can be seen as confused and lacking essential capacities for health. Mixed race people can also project and imagine that others have a more coherent identity, know their place easily and do not suffer from feeling divided, wobbly or conflicted. This may be expressed in fantasies about blood/sex/body – about being mixed and mixed up, about the necessity of a pure identity and that everyone has one bar the mixed race person. As Zadie Smith puts it 'when you come from a mixed race family, it makes you think a bit harder about inheritance and what is passed from generation to generation' (Alibhai-Brown, 2001: 5). There is a particular challenge for the mixed-race child in terms of gaining an identity and placing him/herself within and separate from the parental dyad. Frequently, but not always, the child is a different colour from both its parents, who in turn are a different colour from one another. As children, and adults, we gain our identity from touch, smell, looking and being looked at. So how, as inchoate babies and children, do we make sense of skin colour, and more critically the differences in colour? We are not arguing that children seeing different skin colours feel anxiety, fear, perceive dark colour as that which is alien – these are social meanings. Rather it is important to know what sense is made through differences which are perceived through the tangible effect of different colours within the family – often children within the same family can also be different colours to one another. There can also be the wish to be white with blonde hair and conform to white femininity in order to belong and fit in. For example, Mel B of the Spice Girls pop group and her sister speak about how they wished to be other than they are, wished for paler skin, less frizzy hair, and she adds that this changed over time, and now they have 'learned to love ourselves for being us' (Alibhai-Brown, 2001: 104). Fantasies, needs, wishes shift and fluctuate. What is true at one point cannot be seen as real at another time – truth and what is genuine cannot be pinned down and fixed for all time. Mixed race people, like all others, inhabit social and emotional spheres that are multi-dimensional.

The issue of skin colour and the appreciation of difference of colour are crucial in terms of a person's sense of self and their relationship to self and others. It is commonplace within psychoanalytic theory to argue that the infant forms its relationship to the *Other* – in part through the relationship to touch and to skin. Identity is formed partly through the relationship to skin and provides the boundary between self and other – it is partly the means through which we explore what is inside and outside of the self. Within psychoanalytic object relations theory the boundary between self and other is permeable, in process and never quite in place. Winnicott (1991), elaborated transitional space which is a third area of experience that neither belongs to the inside of the self, the outside of the environment, but rather arises from the social interaction between self and other. It is in this space that all of us, whatever our gendered, classed, ethnicised identity are formed to become who we are. In this third space family differences, family dynamics and the social context are critical for a sense of self and other. It is critical how the parents perceive, respond and think about the child is both similar to, and different from, themselves. Moreover, each child is also different from one another while simultaneously formed through the same family dynamic and processes.

Colonial and racist relations are embedded in the unconscious and permeate our responses and feelings towards self and other, fantasy life – conscious and unconscious. The work of Fanon (1967; 1970) has been influential in developing understandings of colonial subjectivity and the endurance of racism. Fanon's work focused on the effect of colonisation on the colonised and the coloniser. Fanon emphasised how whiteness is internalised and taken into the heart of the self to form our vexed perceptions of others and ourselves. Fanon's central and demanding insight is that these relationships and perceptions cannot be sloughed off, do not operate just on the level of the skin but rather we internalise them profoundly. For Fanon sexual relations across the colour divide combine the personal and the colonial, so a black man having sex with a white woman is, at some level, representing black subjects exacting retribution on white colonialists. A recent article by Shannon Sullivan (2003) uses Laplanche's conceptualisations of how the unconscious is formed to explore how racism is deeply structured in psychic lives. Thoughtfully bringing together Fanon and Laplanche (a French psychoanalyst), Sullivan explores how the very first responses to the infant's body constitute its unconscious life. It is through parental care and the fantasies that are transmitted to the infant through touch and communication that the parent transmits to the infant messages about the infant's body. As Sullivan puts it, 'the adult world is sending unconscious enigmatic messages to children all the time, and it is these messages – not the mere transparent, consciously intended ones – that have the greatest psychosomatic effect on children because they metabolise into unconscious remnants that have a potentially lifelong impact on how children will interact with the world' (Sullivan, 2003: 23).

In Alibhai-Brown's *Mixed Feelings* mothers spoke about feeling proud of their children's colour, and enjoying their children's skin, others expressed shame that they had a 'dark' child, and one mother declared 'I did not want a child who looked too black' (Alibhai-Brown, 2001: 137). Parents who cross a social and cultural taboo to inhabit and participate in a mixed race relationship can be seen as a source of pride for their children, a source of puzzlement – why did they do so? or resentment – why have you put me through this? As issues of loyalty, belonging and identification are always troublesome, the mixed race child may perceive these emotional matters as more difficult. This may especially be the case, if the family dynamics are such that the matters of race, culture and belongingness are used as points of emotional negativity. Included in the dynamic is parental desire and sexual relations. Parents desired another who is perceived within the dominant social order as someone other than themselves. They desired someone either paler or darker than themselves and children have to locate themselves within this dynamic of desire of difference. Fantasies and feelings forge relationships with self and other; they are not free-floating or abstract but rather are stubborn and subtle. People may respond positively to the crossing of a taboo and perceive it as exciting, or other more troubled feelings may be involved.

Identification is partly formed through relationships within and outside of the family. Identification too draws its pulse from fantasy, and is driven by feelings. As Cohen (1994), argues, narratives of fictional families are built up from the imaginary. All children are inextricably engaged in acts of the imagination, fantasise that they have different and superior parents, that they are the King or Queen of the Castle. In the imagination and through their stories they move around trying on different identities, rejecting others, playing with this and that. They live a life of pretence alongside knowing what is real. Children from about the age of six know about the complexity of living, and with increasing awareness are cognisant of the intricacy of human relatedness, about the push-and-pull of reality. There is too strong a predisposition to take what is reported as first the only issue at stake, second that experience can be measured and interpreted, and third that a feeling or a fantasy can have only one meaning. Understanding is not gained by falling down on one side or another, and the truth is not guaranteed by adopting some superior third position. '...rather it consists in recognising that meanings are produced precisely through the interplay of oppositions, and hence are not fixed or unequivocal but always subject to negotiation and revision' (Cohen, 1994: 44). Black children are just as likely to imagine imaginary white companions or peers or heroes, and this does not mean that they are damaged or that they do not know that they are black, are not aware of how they are and may be treated. As Cohen goes on to argue; 'The fact that children can make up tall stories about themselves, featuring imaginary kinships with other races or classes is not necessarily a sign that they are suffering from 'identity confusion' or 'a failure to choose appropriate role models'; on the contrary it can indicate that their powers of imagination have not been damaged beyond repair' (Cohen, 1994: 71). This points to a fundamental issue for the whole debate about identity development in mixed race children – that we should be very wary about making judgements about what is 'normal' and what is 'pathological' in terms of identity development.

Identity Development

Part of the difficulty is the strong tendency to view issues of identity development as linear and straightforward, involving clear-cut cognitive and behavioural processes.

Development, however, is not linear – as human beings we move back, forward and across temporal zones; we identify with different people at various periods in our lives; our needs, feelings and fantasies are diverse and intricate. To develop any racial identity involves awareness, knowledge, confusion, acceptance, and integration (and not necessarily in that order). It critically also involves the social and family context, a child growing up in one context will experience different issues from another child from the same background growing up in a different situation. How people respond and react tends to be different in cities rather than the countryside; in rural Britain children can and do suffer racism, alienation and dislocation frequently through being the only child of colour in their class or school situation. An example is quoted by Alhibi-Brown: 'Ngiao was bright, confident and well liked by her teachers in the metropolis until she moved with her mother to the countryside and then 'she became withdrawn and inarticulate. Her teachers complained that she was attention seeking. Her local doctor assumed she was adopted. She started bed-wetting and was bullied endlessly. The school told her mother that it was her 'aggressive stance more appropriate to an inner city ghetto' which was the problem, not the racism her child was facing. They moved to Bristol and Ngiao is thriving' (Alibhai-Brown, 2001: 108).

Virtually all the discussions on the development of identity, and in particular the identity of mixed race children, portray a mature identity as one in which individuals are at peace with themselves and with others and have settled on an identity which they feel comfortable with, and which they portray to others. Erikson's (1980) 8-stage developmental model is the archetypal model for these theories of the development of identity, and later stage-based theories refer either explicitly or implicitly to Erikson's model. The model postulates a challenge at each of the eight stages, and in order to progress to the next stage, the individual must first overcome the challenge of the previous one.[2]

Erikson and the subsequent stage-based identity theorists acknowledge that confusion, pain and misunderstanding may well be part of the process of identity development, but that by the time adults have attained a mature identity they should no longer experience confusion or distress about their identities. People with mature identities are subject to racism and other distressing events or situations in their lives, but they will have developed resilience to these external challenges due to an inner

---

[2] The 8 Stages are:

- Trust versus Mistrust – Birth to 1 year old
- Autonomy versus Shame and Doubt – 1 year old to 3 years old
- Initiative versus Guilt – 3 years old to 5 years old
- Industry versus Inferiority – 6 years old to 12 years old
- Identity versus Identity Confusion – 12 years old to 21 years old
- Intimacy versus Isolation – Early adulthood
- Generativity versus Stagnation – Middle adulthood
- Integrity versus Despair – greater than 60 years old

sense of self-fulfilment. In this way, the social and political context is by-passed and responsibility for resilience and maturity rests squarely with the individual.

One of the most quoted stage based theories for the development of racial identity is Cross's (1971, 1991) 5-stage model of the development of Nigrescence in Afro-Americans. The five stages are Pre-encounter, Encounter, Immersion/Emersion, Internalisation, and Internalisation/Commitment. Like Erikson, Cross's theory posits the idea that there is an end point to identity (and racial) development, in this case internalisation of and commitment to Nigrescence.

The stage based theory of identity, whilst still common in social work literature on race, has been supplanted in most academic spheres by much more fluid and multi-faceted theories about identity and its development (Giddens, 1991; Parker and Song, 2001). In particular the view that there is an end point to identity such as maturity or Nigrescence, is now seen as a potentially misleading fantasy. Some people, under propitious circumstances, may achieve this position, but for most people racial identity is likely to be an ongoing issue throughout their lives. The expectation that there is a relatively straightforward and easy resolution of identity issues is a denial of the reality of the constant (normal) struggle for identity of the majority of adults from minorities. In fact Cross himself changed his view to a (life cycle) approach where development is seen as an ongoing process rather than a process with a fixed end point.

A more fundamental challenge to the conventional view of racial identity development is provided by Root (1992). Root goes beyond even the life cycle approach in three ways. Firstly she places racial identity development firmly within the context of personal identity development – she argues that gender, class, disability, sexual orientation, culture, are all aspects of identity development, and racial identity cannot be separated from these other components of the whole. Secondly she argues that identity development should not be seen only in personal terms. The nuclear and extended family and the community context need to be taken into account when considering identity development.

One dimension of family functioning which affects racial identity development is the degree of openness which the extended family displays towards accommodating members of other cultures or races. Racism exists within families and communities, and individuals may be marginalised from their own group. As Root puts it: 'multiracial people experience a 'squeeze' of oppression *as* people of colour and *by* people of colour' (Root, 1992: 5). Family and community systems are crucial in terms of the development of mixed race identity.

Root argues that not only can identity change over time, but that at any one time an individual may occupy a number of roles or identities to suit the situation (situational ethnicity). So for example a child may feel perfectly at home with both sets of grand-parents, and behave in a culturally appropriate manner in each of their homes. She may have yet another identity at school, and a further identity with close friends. The orthodox Eriksonian view would be that children who display inconsistent identities must be 'mixed up' and have not therefore successfully overcome the challenge of identity versus role confusion, but Root sees adaptability as a psychological strength rather than as a sign of weakness or confusion. In particular she denies that multiethnic children have to choose between two polar identities, and that choosing one identity of necessity requires a rejection of the other. It is also the case that issues other than race may matter to a child, and that people may wish to identify with the same class, religion or community. Whilst 'race' and ethnicity may be important, they are not necessarily dominant.

By theorising racial identity development as part of an ecological system, Root's theory is in line with contemporary theorising about child development and social problems, as expressed, for example by the *Framework for the Assessment of Children in Need and Their Families* (DoH, 1999). Root goes beyond mere theorising. Like many of the protagonists in this debate (Maximé, 1993; Small, 1992; Dominelli, 1993) Root's theory is not merely a description of the development of identity but contains a moral prescription as to the type of identity that is desirable. Unlike the orthodox theorists however, she positively advocates the right of mixed race/multiethnic people to self-definition and utterly rejects any notion that group or political considerations should proscribe identity. She sees Mixedness as a positive choice, but also allows for choice of one or more ethnic definitions. Her 'Multiethnic Bill of Rights' is a succinct expression of her position:

- Multiracial individuals have the right to self-definition.
- Multiracial individuals must resist the oppressiveness of choosing only one heritage group.
- The right to be complex, ambiguous, and to change over time and situations.
- The right to claim membership in multiple heritage groups.
- The right to prioritise membership with one group.
- The right not to justify cultural classification.

Although Root (1992) incorporates variability and multiplicity into her model, it is based on the assumption that children can choose from a range of identities and decide to adopt the identity, which suits them at that particular moment. We would argue, with Parker and Song (2001) that there are problems with this assumption. Firstly, it may be very difficult to tell whether a particular identity in a specific situation is 'chosen' or 'imposed' on an individual. A mixed race child may behave 'white' with one group of friends and 'black' with another because of quite subtle, possibly unconscious, messages she is getting from these friends about what they expect of her.

These dynamics may never approach overt racism or prejudice, but may play an important part in determining behaviour, feelings and fantasies. They may also have a significant impact on whether or not a child or adult has any active choices. Some situations may be less benign, and the constraint to behave in one way or the other may be even more pressing. These constraints could be intra-psychic (she may have internalised a particular view of herself which is difficult to shift), personal (e.g.

grandparents strong expectation to speak one language or another) or contextual (e.g. having to 'pass for white' in Apartheid South Africa or USA).

Harris (2001), who conducted a study of the racial identity of people in the USA confirms both the fluidity of identity, but also its dependence on contextual factors:

> *Our analysis...provides strong support for the claim that race is socially constructed. Our work shows that adolescent racial identities are quite fluid, with more than 10% of youth expressing different racial identities between the school and home interviews...We provide evidence that context affects race. When forced to choose a single race, the responses of white/black youth are sensitive to the racial composition of their neighbourhoods.*

(Harris, 2001: 20)

Root's (1992) theory can in many ways be classed with those approaches, which celebrate mixed identities and minimise the tension and struggle, which mixed race people may go through in the course of their lives. Whilst her bill of rights is empowering and affirmative for mixed race people, like all the other prescriptive models it could also be disempowering. Whether the 'formula' for successful identity formation is a healthy black identity, a mixed identity or a complex and ambiguous process, all these models imply that there is a path to fulfilment, which can be achieved with relatively little pain. This attitude can give the unconscious message to a child that unless they adhere to the particular formula, there is something wrong with them. Thus the whole raison d'être for these formulae, to empower children and adolescents, can backfire.

Professional/Political Context

The current debates and interventions are of course not occurring in a neutral social and professional context. For example, the Macpherson Inquiry into the death of Stephen Lawrence was a watershed in its acknowledgement that many of the public services, especially the police, are institutionally racist. Whilst this has not led to immediate changes it has opened the debate in ways that had previously been confined to social care, education, academics and welfare professionals. The public tended to be engaged only when they were personally involved or politically motivated. It cannot be assumed, however, that because people are more aware of the issues of racism that they are really engaged with the subject.

Another change has been in the professional discourses that centre on race and ethnicity. In the 1980s the dominating professional discourse revolved around anti-racism and anti-discrimination. In the late 1970s and early 1980s there was intense debate – for example, Ahmed et al. (1986), about interracial adoption and the consequences on black children who were adopted within white families. While these discourses still hold, the current preferred discourse is on 'valuing diversity'. The rationale behind this shift in language and emphasis is that it is preferable to value each individual's contribution to the workplace or society rather than focus attention on particular groups who can then become pigeonholed as oppressors or victims. Further, the argument runs that diversity allows a more open space for the exploration and understanding of our differences and similarities to one another, while the emphasis on difference reinforces divisions between people. Diversity is therefore an attempt to move from the dualities of the 1980s into a much more fluid and complex understanding of social relationships. The language of diversity stresses issues of freedom to choose and is not so hidebound to pathology. However, the ideology of diversity can ignore matters of conflict and tension and it can come close to a 'melting pot' ideology where difference is seen as merely superficial. In fact there are genuine conflicts of interest and cultural tensions between different groups of people. Diversity is also a way of individualising a problem that could be seen as fundamentally an issue of power relations between different groups of people.

Although the trend towards pathologising, psychologising and individualising social problems is a phenomenon of our times, this tendency is particularly prevalent in the social care professions, which, after all were set up to address problems at the interface of the personal and the social. Once mixed race identity is seen as a personal problem, then the logic of intervention becomes clear – the task of the worker is to help the person with the problem to attain fulfilment and maturity. The covert, and at times overt, agenda is for the worker to rescue the individual from their painful and difficult situation by helping them overcome the identity 'problem' at the root of their psychological distress. The operative assumption is that if the child expresses pain, confusion or low self-esteem then they need therapy from an identity expert. Whilst this response is understandable, it does make some assumptions about mixed race identity that have consequences for the individuals concerned. The fantasy that there is a 'mature' or 'resolved position always available' and that the individual can be helped to achieve this drives much of the professional literature, but this may tell us more about the professional ethos and values than it does about the needs and desires of the children involved. Also by being 'child focused' to the exclusion of the family and community context, these interventions are at risk of being counter productive.

On the other hand to say that each case is different and complex can also be an abdication of responsibility and thought. We are not arguing that the understanding of development should be value free. Nor are we asserting that professionals should never intervene, or that race should be ignored. On the contrary complexity is not a reason for not acting and race and racism in the family and the community should be addressed whenever it occurs. Racism, both at an individual and institutional level can severely blight the lives of mixed race children and their families. These children can be even more vulnerable than other ethnic minority children because their families are often isolated and are less likely to be able to access support from either community. Racism should be dealt with as an issue in its own right rather than because it will cause identity confusion and low self-esteem. It can't be combated by the child choosing one or other identity. Indeed Tikly et al. (2004), found that the assumption of identity confusion by teachers is a factor leading to the relatively poor educational attainment of mixed race children.

The plight of mixed race children in the looked after, education and criminal justice systems is indeed a cause of great concern (Barn, 1994; YJB, 2004), however, there should not be a conflation between the issues embroiled in mixed race identity, and those in these systems. As Gilroy (1994), has argued the ruthlessly 'positive' images that were summoned up as an antidote to pathology suggested both intellectual and political weakness and were dearly bought at the price of an aching silence on a whole range of key issues in childcare policy. Gilroy goes on to state that:

> *The assumptions that gave rise to pathology in the first place were not answered but inverted, and then deployed to animate a pastoral image of black family life which would lead a gullible observer to conclude that merely possessing the approved characteristics could also inoculate the community as a whole against abuse, stress and dysfunctionality. In a racist society the opposite conclusion is more likely to be true. Racism itself should be recognised as a factor in increasing household stresses and conflicts about money, status and power, gender and generations. Cultural sameness and common bodily characteristics do not, by themselves, promote good parenting. This is an area in which no guarantees are possible.*
>
> (Gilroy, 1994: xi)

Conclusion

There is an increasing tendency in the social sciences and social care professions to view social forces such as the power relationships between groups, poverty and exclusion as psychological attributes or problems of individuals. The result of this way of viewing the world is to 'psychologise' what are essentially social phenomena. That is why the debates about racism have become focused so much on identity. Identity is about individual subjectivity and personal relations. The focus on identity means that there is less attention given to the social and economic context in which mixed race people live. The focus on individual psychological problems gives the message that mixed race people are the problem which needs sorting out – whether by therapy or by 'celebrating' their identity. Whilst identity is important (and to some people it is the issue that dominates their lives) we need to go beyond identity to understand the social reality of mixed race people and see it as a social phenomenon.

A holistic theory of identity development in mixed race children would have to take into account:

- The global development of the child and their overall identity development.
- Cultural issues (food, music etc.) how they are brought into the family and how they interact with race.

- Family structure and dynamics, including the unconscious racialisation of family processes.
- The extended family and their acceptance of difference within the family.
- The community and neighbourhood context.
- The wider social context and how it changes from time to time.
- Moral or ethical views on the politics of race.

A number of different futures are possible but essentially there are three directions in which racial identity in the UK can develop. Firstly, there could be the continuation of (or development of) the process by which minority ethnic groups, including mixed race, become more coherently a single group, developing a recognisable 'black British' identity and culture. This would mean a continuing and possibly increasing split in the country on black/white lines. This scenario will inevitably lead to more racial tension, but provides the possibility of black and minority ethnic groups becoming a more powerful and unified force in British society, with enough of a critical mass to make real changes. The second possible future would be the development of a mixed race culture that is separate from both black and white and has its own identity. If this happens mixed race people will positively identify as 'mixed' and may eventually become a recognisable group. This could be a positive development for mixed race people offering a distinctive voice and identity and not just the possibility of being between two cultures or a minor part of one culture. However, the danger would be that there would still be struggle and confusion about who would count as mixed race and who would not, so there would be some people on the margins of the margins.

Thirdly and finally, the most likely future development is that there will be no overall pattern. There will be continued fragmentation and diversity with no specific identity but a range of short term situational identities at the individual and group level, depending on current political views, location, family circumstances etc. Whilst this state of affairs does not offer any easy solutions for the identity issue, and holds out the prospect of continuing struggle and debate, it also holds out the possibility for mixed race individuals and groups to take more control of their own lives and identities without being pigeonholed by the agendas of more powerful groups in society.

References

Ahmed, S., Cheetham, J. and Small, J. (1986) *Social Work with Black Children and Their Families.* London: Batsford, BAAF.

Alibhai-Brown, Y. (2001) *Mixed Feelings: The Complex Lives of Mixed Race Britons.* London: Women's Press.

Asthana, A. (2004) The Invisible Colour Between Black and White. London: *The Observer*, 11 July 2004.

Banks, N. (1992) Techniques for Direct Identity Work with Black Children. *Adoption and Fostering*, 16: 3. BAAF.

Barn, R. (1994) *Black Children in Public Care System.* London: BAAF.

Cohen, P. (1994) Yesterday's Words, Tomorrow's Word: From the Racialisation of Adoption to the Politics of Difference, in Gaber, I. and Aldridge, J. (1994) (Eds.) *The Best Interests of the Child: Culture, Identity and Transracial Adoption.* London: Free Association Books.

Cross, W.E. (1971) The Negro to Black Conversion Experience: Toward a Psychology of Black Liberation. *Black World,* 20: 13–27.

Cross, W. (1991). *Shades of Black, Diversity in African American Identity.* Philadelphia: Temple University Press.

Dominelli, L. (1988) *Anti-Racist Social Work.* Basingstoke: Macmillan/BASW.

Erikson, E. (1980) *Identity and the Life Cycle.* London: Norton.

Fanon, F. (1967) *The Wretched of the Earth.* Harmondsworth: Penguin.

Fanon, F. (1970) *Black Skins, White Masks.* London: Paladin.

Frieben-Blum, E., Jacobs, K. and Wießmeier, B. (2000) (Eds.) *Wer ist fremd? Eth-nische Herkunft, Familie und Gesellschaft.* Berlin: Opladen.

Giddens, A. (1991) Modernity and Self-Identity. Cambridge: Polity Press.

Gilroy, P. (1994) Foreword to Gaber, I. and Aldridge, J. (1994) (Eds.) *In the Best Interests of the Child: Culture, Identity and Transracial Adoption.* London: Free Association Books.

Harris, D. (2001) *An Empirical Look at the Social Construction of Race: The Case of Multiracial Adolescents.* Michigan, University of Michigan.

Holland, R. and Holland, K. (1984) Depressed Women: Outposts of Empire and Castles of Skins, in Richards, B. (1984) (Ed.) *Capitalism and Infancy Essays on Psychoanalysis and Politics.* London: Free Association Books.

Maximé, J. (1993) The Importance of Racial Identity for the Psychological Well-being of Black Children. *Association for Child Psychology and Psychiatry Review and Newsletter.* 15: 4.

Park, R. (1928) Human Migration and the Marginal Man. *American Journal of Sociology,* 5.

Parker, D. and Song, M. (Eds.) (2001) *Rethinking 'Mixed Race'.* London: Pluto Press.

Phinney, J.S. (1996) Understanding Ethnic Diversity: The Role of Ethnic Identity. *American Behavioral Scientist,* 40: 143.

Prevatt-Goldstein, B. (1999) Direct Work with Black Children with One White Parent, in Barns, R. (Ed.) *Working with Black Children and Adolescents in Care.* London: BAAF.

Root, M. (1992) *Racially Mixed People in America.* London: Sage.

Rustin, M. (1991) *The Good Society and the Inner World: Psychoanalysis, Policy and Culture.* London: Verso.

Small, J. (1986) Transracial Placements: Conflicts and Contradictions, in Ahmed, S., Cheetham, J. and Small, J. *Social Work with Black Children and Their Families.* London: Batsford/BAAF.

Small, J. (1992) Ethnic and Racial Identity in Adoption within the United Kingdom. *Adoption and Fostering,* 16: 4, 16–21.

Stonequist, E.V. (1937) *The Marginal Man: A Study in Personality and Culture Conflict.* New York: Charles Scribner's Sons.

Sullivan, S. (2003) Enigma Variations: Laplanchean Psychoanalysis and the Formation of the Raced Unconscious. *Radical Philosophy*, 122, Nov/Dec.

Tikly, L., Caballero, C., Haynes, J. and Hill, J. (2004) *Understanding the Educational Needs of Mixed Heritage Pupils.* London: DfES.

Wilson, A. (1987) *Mixed Race Children.* London: Allen and Unwin.

Winnicott, D.W. (1991) *Playing and Reality.* London: Routledge.

Youth Justice Board (2004) *Differences or Discrimination: The Summary of the Report on Minority Ethnic Young People in the Youth Justice System.* London: YJB.

Chapter 5

Identity and Identification: How Mixed Parentage Children Adapt to a Binary World

Toyin Okitikpi

Introduction

The experience of children of mixed parentage continues to be of interest to social commentators, academics and social welfare professionals, Alibhai-Brown, 2001; Olumide, 2002; Barn, 1999; Banks, 2002; Owusu-Bempah, 2000; Tizard and Phoenix, 1993; Song, 2003. As well as discussions about how the children should be classified (categorised), both in official documents and more generally in society, there are also concerns about the children's identity and whether it is possible for them to develop an integrative, multicultural, multiethnic identity and adapt in a race-based, ethnically and culturally diverse social environment. In this chapter I want to suggest that children of mixed parentage are indeed able to adapt and develop a positive sense of identity despite living in social environments that attempt to force a particular identity on them. From the outset I would argue that the starting point from which discussions about the children's identity is conducted is based on a flawed premise. The result of the flawed premise is that the approaches taken towards the children and their families by social workers and other welfare professionals are more likely to cause emotional and psychological damage than the mere fact of being of mixed parentage.

In essence I am arguing that work with children of mixed parentage needs to be less driven by sectarian politics and be more inclusive and integrative in approach. The plea is for an approach that is borne out of the desire to consider what is in the best interest of the children and their families rather than an attempt at social engineering by welfare professionals. Also I would like to suggest that children from mixed parentage background are acutely aware of the complex nature of *difference*, since they are constantly confronted with the daily realities of living in a multi-cultural family environment. It is being suggested that children of mixed parentage are capable of developing a more sophisticated notion of identity than they are sometimes given credit for.

Accepting the fact

During a private conversation about writing a chapter for this volume, Illan Katz opined that the debate about how children of mixed parentage should be classified has already been won, since it is now widely accepted by both the government and welfare authorities that the dual heritage of such children needs to be acknowledged. Moreover, it is no longer deemed acceptable to assume that all children of mixed parentage have to be subsumed under the black or 'other' category in ethnic monitoring forms and other official documents. Indeed Katz noted that the legitimacy and social acceptance of a mixed race group is complete since a mixed race category was included in the 2001 census form. The inclusion of the category at last gave people of mixed parentage the opportunity, should they wish, to choose from a wider list of categories.

Of course, at some level, Katz is quite correct in his assertion that the inclusion of a mixed race category in official documents suggests a certain degree of acceptance and legitimacy of people of mixed parentage, but like all areas pertaining to race, identity, ethnicity and culture, there is often a yawning gap between academics and social commentators' acceptance of a term and wider public acceptance and usage of the same term. The same difficulty can be found in the continuing use of the word 'race' when the discussion is about cultural differences and ethnicity. The use of race, when discussing differences between black and white people, could be argued to reinforce the earlier discourse about racial categorisation, scientific racism and the belief in a world that is easily divisible along racial lines, Tizard and Phoenix, 1993; Jahoda, 1999, Kohn, 1996.

In my view the premise that informs current thinking and discussion about children of mixed parentage is heavily influenced by the race discourse. Taking their cue from a distorted and limited notion of race, there is a false belief amongst some commentators (Banks, 1992, Prevatt-Goldstein, 1999), that the world can be easily divided, primarily, into two groups, black and white. But unlike Pinker's (2002), suggestion of the need to embrace human differences and acknowledge the diversity that exists, Bank's and Prevatt-Goldstein's approach is somewhat reductive and limited because it fails to take account of the diversity that exists and the social and personal realities of individual's experiences.

The historical explanation for dividing the world into such crude and simplistic groupings can be traced back to the earlier period when black people were dominated and condemned to a life of subjugation and slavery (Fryer, 1984). Although I would maintain that there has been a dramatic change in black people's political and social condition from the early period, the legacy of slavery and colonialism still create a powerful impression in the minds of black people in Britain. There is a sense that each new generation of black people experience, and vicariously relive, the pain and powerlessness of their forebears. As each individual person absorbs the realisation that at one point in history their ancestors, and by implication themselves, were deemed as sub-human and held in slavery and servitude for centuries there is an awakening of a consciousness that ignites a rage and a need for the individual to redefine their racial and cultural boundaries. The deep emotional and psychological hurt that this historical legacy evokes together with the continuing experiences of racism in its contemporary form provides the backdrop from which to understand the present. The combination of these experiences provides the 'background noise' that informs all discussion about race, culture, ethnicity and identity. It is this that fuels the discussions about children of mixed parentage and contributes towards the strong, and often negative views, other people hold about the children in general and, inter-racial relationships in particular (Okitikpi, 2002).

The difficulty with current binary perception and approach is that, rather than using history as a springboard for developing a different kind of present and future (a kind of one plus one equals three approach), it is used to set a racial boundary or an imaginary 'front-line' between, what is considered to be, old enemies and it provides further opportunity to settle unfinished business between black and white people.

Also, the other difficulty with a binary worldview is that it takes little or no account of multi-dimensionality because in a binary world people are assigned a racial category and their self-identity, their ethnicity, their cultural background and their community affiliations are thus set accordingly. In my view to take a binary approach is to fail to appreciate the social realities of people's experiences and their ability to transcend their history and reshape their lives in a different way.

The Intolerance of the Oppressed

It is perhaps unsurprising to discover that those who are brutalised and oppressed not only know how oppression and discrimination work but also how to effectively apply similar techniques to others. In my view discussions about the negative views people hold about children of mixed parentage tends to be one sided with very little said or reported about the views and opinions held by black people about the children in general, and the vehement disapprobation of interracial relationships by black women in particular. In essence any discussion about children of mixed parentage that does not acknowledge that which is widely known, but only uttered quietly in private, risk perpetuating and reinforcing the delusion that black people are more tolerant of children of mixed parentage than white people. Banks (2002) hinted at this in his discussion on the experiences of mixed race children and their families but he did not elaborate on it, perhaps for very good reasons. Acknowledging this point is not to imply that all black people are intolerant or, indeed, that white people are more tolerant. However, it is important to understand that for many people of mixed parentage their experience is one whereby they face as much hostility from black people as they do from white people yet there is a silence or lack of comment about how black and white people are both implicated in their negative and oppressive attitudes towards people of mixed parentage. People of mixed parentage, or anybody else for that matter, who dare to speak out about their experiences often face hostile reactions from people who, ironically, accuse them of being an aero, a coconut, 'racist', pro-white, anti-black, self-hating or plainly confused.

Gorman (2003), in a moving account of the negative reactions she encountered writes:

> *I was told by a member of the Nation of Islam that as a mixed race person, I was the embodiment of plantation master-slave rape. I once edited a lifestyle magazine for black women. Almost immediately after my appointment, I received hate mail from black women who had seen my picture inside the cover. I was called a red skin bitch, a black-hating whore, milky-faced cunt. I left the job three months later.*

(Gorman, 2003: 35)

This is perhaps a different starting point from that which is often presented because in most instances one group, the white majority, are deemed to be the main culprits of oppressing minorities while the other group, black minorities are, because of their position in society, thought to be incapable of being oppressors. In making the point the intention is not to blame the victim or to suggest that the oppression and racism that black people experience is insignificant. The Macpherson Report, the BBC documentary the 'Secret Police' and countless other TV programmes, films and radio broadcasts, and other publications, for example, Fryer, 1984, are compelling evidence of the realities of the black experience of racial oppression in the UK. Rather, the reason for mentioning such unmentionables is to encourage an honest and open discussion and to acknowledge the complexities involved in this area. What Gorman's experience indicates is that when looking at the experiences of children of mixed parentage no one group can claim that they have a greater capacity for tolerance. In work with children of mixed parentage it is simply not the case that black workers, more than white workers, have been more open minded in enabling a child or young person of mixed parentage to develop their uniqueness and given the opportunity to explore their dual heritage. In essence, based on the experiences of people of mixed parentage, both black and white people are very similar in their negative attitudes towards the children and their families, Montague and Alibhai-Brown, 1992; Olumide, 2002 and Owusu-Bempah and Howitt, 2000.

What's Reflected?

When reading works that attempt to explore the experiences of children of mixed parentage and provide suggestions of how best to work with them it soon becomes evident that the racist inspired one-drop rule pervades the approaches being advocated (Banks, 1995, 2002; Maxime, 1986; Prevatt-Goldstein, 1999).

Spencer (1997) observes that:

Many black[s] (people) frown upon the entire multiracial movement and feel that it is simply a lack of self-esteem on the part of the white parents to want their mixed race children to claim a part-white identity alongside their black identity. Blacks feel this way particularly in light of the fact that this racist society will still view mixed race children as black.

(Spencer, 1997: 26)

From a slightly different perspective but still making the same point Prevatt-Goldstein (1998) asserted that:

I would suggest that the desired outcome for a black child with a white parent is that a child feels positive about themselves as a black child with a white parent and feels part of a group that contributes, survives, challenges.

(Prevatt-Goldstein, 1998: 50)

Clearly by referring to a child of mixed parentage as a black child with a white parent, Prevatt-Goldstein feels the need to acknowledge that there is a white parent involved but she is finding it difficult to go the whole way, and she is struggling with the issue of identity and definitions. However, leaving that to one side, the question which is not often asked is, what is a child to do when they look in the mirror and the reflection they see bears no resemblance to the black teacher they see in the nursery or at school, the black parent they live with or the black children they see around them? There seems to be reluctance, on the part of some social welfare professionals, commentators and academics to accept the reality that the children are from inter-racial households and that one of the child's parents is black and the other white. There seems to be an attempt to redress social injustices, oppression and discrimination by ignoring or attempting to re-write the child's white cultural background while glorifying and accentuating the child's black cultural background.

In my view the difficulty with the assertion that because the children live in a culture that idealises whiteness and devalues blackness and therefore they should be encouraged to embrace only their blackness is that it fails to entertain the possibility that children are not mere puppets who are at the mercy of their social environment. Also the assertion puts all the important ingredients for developing identity into a mix (ethnicity, cultural background, social environment, social influences, historical legacies, familial backgrounds, intra-psychic dynamics), but only comes up with one possible outcome, that children of mixed parentage could only be black. What is ignored is that identity formation and what makes individuals feel a sense of pride about who they are and where they feel they belong is both idiosyncratic and complex. Skin colour and how people perceive others are not, in themselves, enough to determine where, how and with whom individuals may choose to identify. For example Benson, although somewhat dated but nevertheless still relevant, found in her study that:

There was no correlation between relative skin colour and problems of identity and only tentative evidence to suggest that girls might be more prone to reject a 'coloured' identity than boys. What was clear, however, was that disturbed children tended to be found in households where the parents had not themselves succeeded in working out a satisfactory social solution to the problems arising from their situation as interracial couples.

(Benson, 1981: 143)

This is an interesting observation, though for a different reason, because it rightly refocuses the problem away from the children towards those around the children, i.e. their parents and carers. Although it is unclear whether Benson subscribes to the view that the children are black, the notion that how the children identify themselves and the degree of difficulty they experience in trying to come to terms with who they are and make sense of their identity and where they belong is greatly influenced, at least in the early stage, by the attitudes and reactions of those around them.

Spickard (2001) also recognised the importance of the facilitative role others have in enabling the children to develop their sense of identity. In a private conversation with Daniel (1999) Spickard reported that:

The telling of one's ethnic story, often a story of trying on various identities, is especially important in the case of a multiracial person who, frequently, it would appear from the reactions expressed by commentators, that children of mixed parentage are not afforded the opportunity to play act with different identities and fantasise about what they could aspire to be or what sort of person they want to become and the kind of relationship they want to develop with the wider world. Instead they are pathologised and they become objects of concern for clinical psychologists to begin work on. As a rule the aim is often to re-programme them so that they embrace the 'right' particular culture and ethnicity.

(Daniel, 1999, reported in Spickard, 2001)

In essence this is a challenge about both the assumptions and assertions that a child of mixed parentage must either be confused about their sense of identity, or they are self-hating and black-hating children who want to (pass) as white.

The Blank Slate Syndrome

The discussion about labelling and finding the correct terminology to use for children of mixed parentage is often clouded by race politics and the low-level on-going culture wars between black and white activists, commentators and academics (Okitikpi, 1999). Also, as Owusu-Bempah observes in Chapter 3, the difficulty with all these labels is that they exclude as much as they include and while some people may be quite happy to be identified under any of the labels that may be in vogue others may find such labels to be crass, inappropriate and, in some cases, offensive. What soon becomes clear in any attempt to categorise people along clearly demarcated racial, ethnic or cultural lines is the sheer complexity of the exercise. Why is it such a surprise that in a tolerant, multicultural, multiethnic and cosmopolitan society, geographical propinquity would lead to a great deal of interethnic and interracial intimate relationships? (Okitikpi, 2002).

In essence, as a result of such 'mixing', any grouping or labelling quickly becomes meaningless because people do not always fit neatly into a pre-ordained category. For example under what category would a child be placed if her mother is of mixed parentage (black Caribbean mother and white Irish father) and her father is white English? Or a child whose father is an Afro-Trinidadian Chinese and mother is Anglo-Asian? What quickly becomes evident in any perfunctory investigation into the labels mixed race or mixed parentage is that the terms are used primarily to denote a child who comes from a background where one parent is black Caribbean or African and the other white, otherwise a child whose mother is black Caribbean and father is black African would also be called mixed race. Of course finding the most appropriate label under which people can be identified need not necessarily be a negative endeavour, however, it is a problem if it becomes a 'Holy Grail'.

There is a certain degree of unreasonableness and lack of logic in the assumptions that are made about children of mixed parentage and in the way these children are viewed. In most instances they are deemed to be devoid of any innate resilience nor are they credited with the ability to transcend their individual circumstance and shape their world differently. They are generally depicted as blank slates who are incapable of being actively involved in shaping their own lives. The world of the mixed race child is assumed to be one in which all known child developmental processes and ideas that apply to all other children are suspended and they are depicted as mere puppets, who are easily manipulated against their true identity by ill informed carers and their white mothers. In reality the picture is more complex and many children struggle to make sense of who they are, where they feel they belong and which people are important to them. Ordinarily these quests for self-identity are accepted as part of a process of maturation that all children, and indeed many adults, go through irrespective of their racial and social backgrounds. This questioning is considered to be part of children's and young people's attempt to make sense of and come to terms with a social and familial world that is both different and the same as themselves. The major difference between children of mixed parentage and other (mono-racial) children is that while other children are afforded the opportunity to 'dress-up' and play around with conflicting identities, children of mixed parentage are deemed to be damaged and that somehow theirs is a confused identity.

To date there is a dearth of materials that ascribe positive attributes to mixed race children and their familial background. Those authors who have challenged assumptions about the children and dared to suggest that the children are perhaps not as confused about their sense of identity as has been reported nor are they psychologically scarred because they are from an interracial background, face disapprobation (Alibhai-Brown, 1993; Tizard and Phoenix, 1993; Spencer, 1997; Katz, 1996).

In general there appears to be very little credit given to the children's ingenuity and their ability to adapt and cope in a social environment that pulls them in different directions and continues to view the world as binary. Many children left to their own devices do not necessarily see their familial environment or their upbringing as negative. Also they may find that the crass assumption by many practitioners that their white parent is incapable of providing them with a culturally mixed upbringing is wide of the mark. Clearly it would be the case that some children of mixed parentage would come from a home background where the father or mother or both are absent and they therefore would play little or no active role in their development and indeed some children would come from abusive, insensitive and indeed racist households. However, it is worth acknowledging that these types of home environment conditions are not just exclusive to children of mixed parentage and the same conditions may also be evident in mono-racial households.

Children of mixed parentage grow up in social and familial environments where they not only see difference and diversity but they are directly and indirectly affected by it. Even in instances where they may choose to take a 'colour blind' approach and ignore all that they see around them, they still have to deal with the negative reactions of other people. They, like black children, are invariably reminded, by the reactions of others, that they are visibly different. In various situations with other children and adults, children of mixed parentage have reported that their colouring has been the subject of speculation as people have attempted, wrongly, to identify who they were and where they may have originated. In some cases there is a tendency to attribute exceptional beauty to children of mixed parentage with complements to them describing their colour in a variety of seemingly positive ways. While this may appear positive it could also be interpreted as the continual fetishisation of the children because of their interracial background. These assumptions, negative reactions and attitudes towards the children act as reminders to the children about their place within the wider social environment and that others hold strong views about them because they are from a background where one of their parents is white and the other black.

Being Accommodated

It is now widely accepted that there is a disproportionately higher percentage of children of mixed parentage in care and once in the care system they tend to stay there for a much longer period than other children (Bebbington, 1989; Okitikpi, 1999). Why there is such an over-representation and why, once there, they should be in care for a longer period than other children has been explored elsewhere (Okitikpi, 1999), what is important to note however is that coming from an interracial background makes them more vulnerable to being accommodated into the care system in comparison to other children. While in the care system children of mixed parentage possess the same vulnerability, tenacity, pragmatism and resilience necessary to survive in the care system as other children.

There is an emotional and psychological price that children who are accommodated have to pay when they are taken into the care system. Irrespective of the reasons for their accommodation, children experience feelings that are akin to bereavement, initially at least, as they leave a familiar environment for a new and unfamiliar one. Some children of course are able to thrive in their new environment, because it provides stability, predictability, and consistency and, just as importantly, it contains people who are supportive and caring. However, for some children their new environment is a source of heartache as they find it difficult to comprehend why they are away from their family and living in a strange place with unfamiliar smells, voices and faces. For children of mixed parentage in the care system their sense of isolation and abandonment may be compounded by seeing others successfully placed with adopted families or in long-term placements while they languish in the residential unit waiting for a family.

Protean Style

Kreps and Kunimoto (1994) observe that:

> *Every individual is composed of a unique combination of different cultural orientations and influences, and every person belongs to many different cultural groups. It is important that we recognise the influences of many cultures on our lives. Based on our heritage and life experiences we each develop our own idiosyncratic identity.*

> (Kreps and Kunimoto, 1994: 3)

Kreps and Kunimoto's assertion accepts that an individual's identity is not fixed and that people make use of the different influences around them to forge their own identity. This is an important point because when discussing the experiences and identity of children of mixed parentage there is often a tendency to perceive them as victims of their backgrounds who need to be rescued and reprogrammed. There is a fallacy, in my view, that parents or carers are able to mould their children into whomsoever they desire and that the children are basically passive recipients of an identity that is somehow 'bestowed upon them'. As Pinker suggests, 'That children don't turn out the way their parents want is, for many people, one of the bittersweet lessons of parenthood. Your children are not your children', wrote the poet Kahil Gilbran. 'You may give them your love but not your thoughts, for they have their own thoughts' (Pinker, 2002: 249).

Both Pinker and Kreps and Kunimoto are not suggesting that parents and carers do not have a major influence on the development of their children's identity, on the contrary they do make a significant contribution, however they are but one among a plurality of voices and influences. In essence, far from being 'blank slates', children of mixed parentage are capable of engaging with their social environment in a dynamic way. Many of them recognise that they are neither black nor white since they do see others around them who are (indeed) black and white. Alibhai-Brown and Montague (1992b) explored the issue of categorisation by looking at the experiences of young people of mixed parentage who questioned the black identity that was, in their view, being foisted upon them. Many of the young people they interviewed challenged the ascription of others by asserting 'don't call me black'. In my own interviews with children of mixed parentage about the issue of mixed race identity, a 15-year-old young man (white English mother and black Nigerian father) said that once he had worked through his anger about the assumptions other people make about him and his questioning of the reasons people felt the need to categorise him in the first place, he finally declared that he was neither black nor white but in fact brown. And like many others of mixed parentage he is able to recognise the different claims that are made about him and his identity. Also, like others, there is recognition and an acceptance that he comes from a diverse background with two different sets of grand-parents and extended families. In line with many of the people interviewed for this chapter he was able to identify that there was a great deal of difference within and between each set of grandparents. On his father's side there are people who have been and are involved in relationships with others from different ethnic groups. For example a Yoruba man and a mixed parentage (Nigerian/German) woman, an Indian woman and a Yoruba man, a Itsekiri man with a Yoruba woman and a Hausa Muslim man with a Yoruba Christian woman. On his mother's side there is a white Yorkshire woman with a Chinese man, another woman with an African American man and a white Yorkshire man with an Asian woman. Of course within each family there are also those who have formed relationships with people from the same ethnicity, however what the example illustrates is that some people come from social environ-ments that are not necessarily mono-racial but contain a diversity of people from different ethnic and cultural backgrounds. However, far from viewing such mixed backgrounds as a negative aberration with many disadvantages and far from being wracked by self-hatred, angst and unresolved racial antagonisms, these young people simply saw this as their 'family background' with all the same intrigues and machina-tions that are evident in all other families. As Tizard and Phoenix, 1993; Wilson, 1987 and Alibhai-Brown, 2001, also found, many of the young people I interviewed did not perceive their life or the multiracial/multiethnic mix of their background in the same way as others perceive it. However, unlike my 15-year-old interviewee, many were reluctant, and in some cases afraid, to take the same aggressive approach in chal-lenging the racial category which others are attempting to foist upon them.

Adapting to a Binary World

Concerns about whether children of mixed parentage will develop a positive, inte-grated, identity have a long history (Park, 1937; Stonequist, 1937; Tizard and Phoenix, 1993; Wilson, 1987; Okitikpi, 1999). But Richmond (1954) cited in Wilson (1987) observes:

There is no inherent reason why mixed marriages should not be successful, or why coloured children should not grow up into healthy, well-adjusted citizens. That mixed marriages are less often successful than others, and that the children of such marriages sometimes become severely maladjusted, must be attributed to the widespread existence of colour prejudices and the practice of discrimination.

Wilson also cites Banton's (1955) research conducted in Stepney, London, which caused him to observe that:

It is impossible to say how much the children born of interracially mixed marriages do suffer. In all probability they suffer less on account of the colour factor than on account of the disadvantages entailed by their position in the economic and social structure.

(ibid).

In her study of fifty-one children of mixed parentage Wilson concluded that:

From a litany of tentative statements, based sometimes on scanty evidence, one theme has emerged from this study with certainty: that the view of mixed race children as a 'problem', unable to find security and acceptance from any ethnic group, is outmoded. The idea that mixed race people are, by the very nature of their position, torn by spiritual uncertainty and racked by malaise is an oversimplified anachronism in the multiethnic mosaic which Britain has become. The inadequacy of this 'problem' approach to mixed race children has highlighted a general lack of flexibility in the modern approach to racial category. A dichotomous black-white view of racial categorisation, which is an adequate tool for analysing the racism of white institutions, is too blunt an instrument with which to dissect the intricate contents of a child's racial identity.

(Wilson, 1987: 199)

Children of mixed parentage background don't need to wake up in the morning and look at themselves in the mirror and run to the rooftop to shout that they are *mixed race and proud, or indeed they are brown and proud.* However, it is my contention that because of their backgrounds and their need to move beyond straddling the two opposing camps, the children are capable of developing a racial identity that corresponds to the reality of their background. In other words children from interracial backgrounds are adaptable to their backgrounds and they are capable of developing a multi-cultural and biracial identity because they are able to integrate the different strands of their family backgrounds. So, I would assert that far from being confused about their racial identity, many children of mixed parentage have had to develop the social competence that enables them to negotiate their way through difficult, contradictory and hostile racially divided social environments. In fact, as Spencer (1997) points out:

The narrow black nationalist attitude overlooks the fact that while some mixed race people settle on a monoracial identity, others, as a result of being raised in an interracial home, have fluid identities that adjust to the immediate context. Such a person may feel biracial at home, white amongst accepting white grandparents, and black amongst black relatives or in an all white classroom.

(Spencer, 1997: 29)

In my view Spencer is not suggesting a *chameleon-like* personality, rather he is putting forward the notion that, like others, people of mixed parentage are able to adapt well to their social environment and therefore capable of interacting with others and have the ability to shape the nature of their relationships with the people around them.

As is well documented children are able to notice racial differences from a young age (Clark and Clark, 1939; Milner, 1983), but in order to learn the skills and the ability to adapt to their social environment they need help and support, at least initially, to develop the emotional and psychological foundations that are necessary. In his conclusion Banks (2002) rightly identified that:

The progress the parents make in developing strategies to cope with social hostility and those strategies which they use to discuss differences with their child will help build the child's sense of uniqueness and confidence. This will be necessary for individual psychological security and family relationship development. A family with children of mixed parentage has additional tasks to accomplish to ensure positive psychological development for their children. This task is one that needs open, at ease discussion for children not to feel ill at ease. The parents of mixed parentage children will need to consider their own barriers, if any, to this discussion and move through a process to help them gain additional confidence in achieving the necessary tasks.

(Banks, 2002: 231)

Bank's recognition of the pivotal role that the children's carers and parents could play in helping them to develop a solid foundation from which to build psychological and emotional security is of crucial importance because it suggests that those caring for the children must sort out their own psychological and emotional barriers and accept the fact that the children are from a bi-cultural background.

The contention of this chapter is that children of mixed parentage are capable of forming multiple and meaningful relationships with other children as well as adults. Indeed Young (1990) made the point that: '...our identities are defined in relation to how others identify us, and they do so in terms of groups which are already associated with specific attributes, stereotypes and norms'. (Young, 1990: 46).

But importantly Young recognised the reciprocity and reflexivity involved in identity formation because it was further asserted that; 'From the throwness of group affinity it does not follow that one cannot leave groups and enter new ones...nor does it follow from the throwness of group affinity that one cannot define the meaning of group identity for oneself; those who identify with a group can redefine the meaning and norms of group identity'. (Young, 1990: 46).

Similarly, according to Kich (1992), multiracial people go through three different stages before coming to a state of total self-acceptance. Kich's Stage 1 is an initial awareness of being different and of dissonance between self-perceptions and other people's perception; Stage 2 is multiracial people's wish to be accepted by others; and Stage 3 is a gradual self-acceptance as a multiracial person. For Kich these three stages enable an individual to move; 'from a questioning, questionable, sometimes devalued sense of self to one where an interracial self-concept is highly valued and secure' (Kich, 1992: 305).

Kich's idea of 'multiracial people' is very similar to Song's (2003), notion of 'Panethnic Identities'. Although Song does not elaborate on the intra-psyche processes that people go through as they fuse the multi-dimensionality of their background, there is nevertheless an acknowledgement that it is possible, and indeed desirable, to integrate the different influences that contribute towards the development of an individual's sense of self.

Conclusion

The idea that by dint of their backgrounds children of mixed parentage would automatically experience confusion and difficulties about their sense of identity and that they are incapable to developing a self concept and identity that is integrative continues to characterise the approach taken by many professionals toward these children. The attempt in this chapter has been to urge social welfare professionals, in particular social workers, to think about the extent to which their assumptions about the children's white mothers and their views about intimate interracial relationships influences their approach towards the children. Despite the increasing number of interracial relationships in the UK and the high numbers of children born of one white parent and one black parent (PSI, 1997), there is still a feeling that people treat the relationships and the children from such relationships as something new or a trend that would not last. In my view there is a need for a fresh look at the way the children (and by implication their families) are perceived and a re-evaluation of the assumptions that governs our understanding of their experiences. It is evident that the assumptions that governs the way some social welfare professionals work with the children is greatly influenced by the bad experiences of children from difficult, problematic or dysfunctional backgrounds. In other words there is a tendency to generalise the negative experiences of a particular group of mixed race children to all children of mixed parentage.

It is important to acknowledge that identity formation is not an easy process because it is fraught with complications, elations, discoveries, uncertainties, contradictions and frictions. However, these experiences are part of the process of growing up and the emotional and psychological feelings that are manifested are both negative and positive. But the important point being advanced is that all children go through similar processes and the degree to which they are able to manage the processes successfully is down to a variety of factors, one of which is the attitudes and behaviours of those around them.

References

Alibhai-Brown, J. and Montague, A. (1992). *The Colour of Love: Mixed Race Relationships.* London: Virago.

Alibhai-Brown, J. (2001) *Mixed Feelings: The Complex Lives of Mixed Race Britons.* London: Women's Press.

Alibhai-Brown, J. and Montague, A. (1992b) Don't Call Me Black: Mixed Race Identity Dilemmas. *New Statesman-New Society,* 7 Feb, 14–5.

BBC 1 Television (2004) *The Secret Police.* Panorama Programme.

Banks, N. (1992) Techniques for Direct Work with Black Children. *Fostering and Adoption,* 16: 3, 19–25.

Banks, N. (1995) Children of Black Mixed Parentage and Their Placement Needs. *Adoption and Fostering.* 19: 2, 19–24.

Banks, N. (2002) Mixed Race Children and Families, in Dwivedi, K.N. *Meeting the Needs of Ethnic Minority Children.* London: JKP.

Banton, M. (1955) in Wilson, A. (1987) *Mixed Race Children.* London: Allen and Unwin.

Barn, R. (1999) White Mothers, Mixed Parentage Children and Child Welfare. *British Journal of Social Work.* 29: 269–84.

Bebbington, A. and Miles, J. (1989) *The Background of Children who are Looked-after in Local Authority Care.* London: BAAF.

Benson, S. (1981) *Ambiguous Ethnicity.* Cambridge: Cambridge University Press.

Clark, K.B. and Clark, M.K. (1939) The Development of Consciousness and Self and the Emergence of Racial Identification in Negro Pre-School Children. *Journal of Social Psychology,* 10: 3, 55–67.

Daniel, R.G. – in private conversation with Spickard, P.R.

Fryer, P. (1984) *Staying Power.* London: Routledge.

Jahoda, G. (1999) *Images of Savages: Ancient Roots of Modern Prejudice in Western Culture.* London: Routledge.

Katz, I. (1996) *The Construction of Racial Identity in Children of Mixed Parentage. Mixed Metaphors.* Jessica Kingsley. London.

Katz, I. (1999) *Mixed Metaphors: The Construction of Mixed Race Identity.* London: JKP.

Kich, G.K. (1992) The Developmental Process of Asserting a Biracial, Bicultural Identity, in Rootes, M. *Racially Mixed People in America.* London: Sage.

Kohn, M. (1996) *Race Gallery: The Return of Racial Science.* London: Vintage.

Kreps, G.L. and Kunimoto, E.N. (1994) *Effective Communication in Multicultural Health Care Settings.* London: Sage.

Maxime, J.E. (1986) Some Psychological Models of Black Self Concept, in Ahmed, S., Cheetham, J. and Small, J. (Eds.) *Social Work with Black Children and their Families.* London: Batsford.

Milner, D. (1983) *Children and Race: Ten Years On.* London: Ward Lock Educational.

Okitikpi, T. (1999) Identification of Mixed Race Children. *Issues in Social Work Education,* 19: 1, 93–106.

Okitikpi, T. (2004) *Anti-Discriminatory and Anti-oppressive Practice: Working with Ethnic Minority Children in Foster and Residential Care.* EUSARF.

Olumide, G. (2002) *Raiding the Gene Pool: The Social Construction of Mixed Race.* London: Pluto.

Owusu-Bempah, J. and Howitt, D. (2000) *Psychology beyond Western Perspectives.* Oxford: BPS Blackwell.

Park, R. (1937) Introduction, in Stonequist, E. *The Marginal Man.* New York: Scribners.

Pinker, S. (2002) *The Blank Slate.* London: Penguin.

Prevatt-Goldstein, B. (1999) Direct Work with Black Children with a White Mother, in Barn, R. *Working with Black Children and Adolescents in Need.* London: BAAF.

Policy Studies Institute (1997) *Ethnic Minorities in Britain: Fourth National Survey.* London: PSI.

Richmond A.H. (1954) in Wilson, A. (1987) *Mixed Race Children.* London: Allen and Unwin.

Rootes, M. (1992) *Racially Mixed People in America.* London: Sage.

Song, M. (2003) *Choosing Ethnic Identity.* Cambridge: Polity Press.

Spencer, J.M. (1997) *The New Coloured People: The Mixed Parentage People in America.* New York: University Press.

Spickard, P.R. (2001) The Subject is Mixed Race: The Boom in Biracial Biography, in Parker, D. and Song, M. (Eds) 2001. *Rethinking Mixed Race.* London. Pluto Press.

Stonequist, E. (1937) *The Marginal Man.* New York: Scribners.

Tizard, B. and Phoenix, A. (1993) *Black, White or Mixed Race.* London: Sage.

Wilson, A. (1987) *Mixed Race Children.* London: Allen and Unwin.

Young, I.M. (1990) *Justice and Politics of Difference.* Princeton: PUP.

Chapter 6

Practice Issues: Working with Children of Mixed Parentage

Lena Robinson

Introduction

This chapter will explore issues related to working with children and young people of mixed parentage. In this chapter, the term 'black' will be used specifically to refer to people of African and African Caribbean descent. The terms 'mixed parentage'; 'mixed race' 'dual heritage' 'biracial' are often used to describe first generation offspring of parents of different 'races'. They most typically describe individuals of black and white racial heritage (Sebring, 1985), but are not limited to this combination. In this chapter the terms will refer to individuals, one of whose parents is African Caribbean or Asian (Indian, Pakistani, Bangladeshi) and the other white European.

Identity formation is widely acknowledged as one of the central tasks of adolescence (Erikson, 1968; Marcia, 1980). Erikson (1968), proposed a process whereby adolescents begin with an unclear sense of their identity, experience a 'crisis', and eventually achieve a clear sense of their identity. He felt that 'identity crisis' was normative to adolescence and young adulthood. Scholars 'no longer refer to this process as a 'crisis'…'Exploration' better describes the typical adolescent's gradual, uneventful approach to identity formation' (Berk, 1998: 389).

Identity formation is 'crucial for ethnic minority (mixed parentage) children who face many disparagements to self-esteem from the external world' (Bagley, 1993: 72). As children of mixed parentage increase in the population (see Census, 2001) many will manage to achieve truly integrated identities, while others will experience chronic identity conflicts. This latter group will pose a growing challenge to social work professionals in the 21st century. The issues discussed in this chapter are offered as the initial steps toward an understanding of these issues.

The topic of racial or ethnic identity in mixed parentage children has received increasing attention in recent years (Root, 1992; Tizard and Phoenix, 1993). This interest has been spurred by demographic trends that indicate a rapid increase in the mixed parentage population and by the acknowledgement that there is little well-defined research and theory in the area. According to Berrington (1995), more than one in five of all ethnic minority children in Britain under the age of four years are of mixed parentage. The size of the ethnic minority population was 4.6 million in 2001 or 7.9 per cent of the total population of the United Kingdom. Fifteen per cent of the ethnic minority population described their ethnic origin as mixed and about a third of this group were from white and black Caribbean backgrounds (Census, 2001). The experiences of mixed parentage children and young people will vary, reflecting differences in their class, education and family cultures.

What is known

Reviews of the limited research in Britain suggest that few children seemed to experience their situation as 'a painful clash of loyalties between black and white' (Wilson, 1987; Tizard and Phoenix, 2002). In Tizard and Phoenix's study most of the children had high self-esteem and positive identities. They found that 'a mixed identity was as likely to be positive as a black identity' (Tizard and Phoenix, 1993: 174), and that 'wanting to be white was the major indicator of a problematic identity for mixed parentage adolescents' (Ibid: 162). Tizard and Phoenix (2003) reported that children were as likely to identify themselves as 'mixed' as they were 'black'. 'Even if they were seen as black by others, they experienced themselves as 'mixed'' (Ibid). They acknowledge that black self-identification among children of mixed parentage tends to correlate with the degree of politicisation on issues of 'race' and racism. Their study also found that despite majority 'white' orientations in terms of friendships, racialised conflict situations produced strong black identifications (Ibid).

There are some mixed parentage children whose experiences give cause for concern and these are the children who are up to two-and-a-half times more likely than other children to enter care (Bebbington and Miles, 1989). Recent studies of the placement of black children with permanent families found almost twice as many mixed parentage children as children with two African Caribbean parents (Barn, 1990; Charles, Rashid and Thoburn, 1992). Studies have shown that some mixed parentage (children and) adolescents in local authority care exhibit identity confusion and low self-esteem (Banks, 1992; Maxime, 1993; Barn, Sinclair and Ferdinand, 1997). Researchers have often conjectured that mixed parentage children are at risk for developing a variety of problems (Stonequist, 1937; Porterfield, 1978). Potential problems include cultural and racial identification issues, lowered self-esteem, difficulties in dealing with conflicting cultural demands and feeling marginal in two cultures.

A long-held notion is that mixed parentage individuals who are the offspring of one white parent and one African, African Caribbean or Asian parent, should identify with only one racial or ethnic group, specifically with the group of the black parent (Root, 1996). Some authors (Small, 1986; Maxime, 1993) argue that mixed parentage children and youngsters should be classified as black and that they should see themselves as so. Small (1986: 92), points out that 'in this society (United Kingdom) any child who has the slightest taint of black is seen by the white majority as black'. Denial of a child's ethnic roots by white parents was said to give the child 'a white mask', and prevent 'exposure to his or her own self' (Small, 1986: 92). The argument is that society sees them as black and they will be better off if that is their self-perceived identity. This tendency is related to the 'one-drop rule' (see Chapter 5 of this volume, for a detailed discussion) and in indeed, some United States studies, 'mixed white and Afro-American children are regarded as black, and not studied separately' (Tizard and Phoenix, 1989: 431). Today, most researchers (see Root, 1996 and Chapter 5 this volume), argue that the one-drop solution is not a useful way to categorise mixed-parentage people. They propose the creation of a category for mixed parentage people that acknowledges them as separate and distinct from black and white people.

Finding a positive identity

Although mixed parentage children and youngsters encounter the problems faced by most minorities, they must also figure out how to reconcile the heritages of both parents in a society that categorises individuals into single groups. Thus, if a person wants to achieve a positive biracial identity, they have to take in and value both racial parts of themselves. However, the development of a healthy biracial identity:

> *Means not only accepting and valuing both (black and white) heritages and being comfortable in both the minority and majority community, but having the flexibility to accept that others may identify them as minority, majority or biracial.*
>
> (Pinderhughes, 1995: 81)

Wilson (1987) writes:

> *It seems to me desirable that mixed race children accept both sides of their dual heritage, provided that in doing so they do not lose sight of the fact that white society sees them as black and metes out to them the same degree of disadvantage that it does to all black people.*
>
> (Wilson, 1987: vii)

Carter argues that: 'a person who is biracial should become grounded in the devalued (black) racial group as a foundation for facilitating the merger of the two racial groups. This is particularly true for racial groups in the United States (and Britain)' (Carter, 1995: 120). According to Carter: 'when one has first developed a positive black identity and uses the black identity as a foundation, it allows incorporation of the white aspect of identity' (Carter, 1995: 120). In a study of racial identity attitudes of mixed parentage (African Caribbean/white) adolescents in Britain, Fatimilehin (1999), used the RIAS-B scale (Parham and Helms, 1981), to investigate the attitude of these youngsters to their black heritage. Fatimilehin found that older teenagers were more likely to have positive racial identity attitudes and a positive relationship was found between racial identity attitudes and self-esteem. However, monoracial models of minority identity development do not address all the issues facing mixed parentage adolescents. For example, Cross's (1978) model includes rejection of the minority culture followed by rejection of the majority culture and does not include the possibility of integrating more than one racial/ethnic group identity into one's sense of self. Various authors (Poston, 1990; Kerwin and Ponterotto, 1995) have therefore argued that there is a need to develop models of biracial identity development.

Several models of biracial identity development have been proposed (e.g., Jacobs, 1992; Kerwin and Ponterotto, 1995; Kich, 1992; Poston, 1990; Root, 1992). These authors questioned the applicability of monoracial identity models to those of biracial heritage. Many of these frameworks demonstrate a similar hierarchy of stages that begin with initial learning about race and ethnicity differences, move to the struggle to find an identity but feeling pressured to choose only one group, and finally end in achievement of some level of biracial identity where both cultures are accepted and integrated into the person's overall identity. Root (1990) is the exception here. She describes four different paths that individuals can choose, all of which can lead to a positive biracial existence. Her possible outcomes include choosing the identity assigned by others, identifying with both racial groups, choosing one racial group over the others, and identifying with a new, biracial or multiracial group. Although Root (1990) describes how an individual can be successful with any of these choices, her model, like many of the others, implies that the latter of the solutions is possibly the most beneficial. All of these models differ from Stonequist's (1937) early deficit conceptualisation of biracial individuals who suffer marginalised existences because they never live fully in either culture of their background.

Myth making

In an article that reviewed the theories about mixed parentage identity formation Kerwin and Ponterotto (1995), outlined the following myths regarding mixed parentage children: the stereotype that biracial children are marginal persons; the myth that mixed parentage individuals must choose to identify with only one group; that mixed parentage children do not want to discuss their racial identity. Important variables to consider with these children are that they may choose one group over the other at different stages of their life (Poston, 1990) and that these choices are often influenced by their social and family situation and exposure, the composition and nature of their peer group, their participation in cultural activities, their physical appearance and language facility, intergroup tolerance, and their sense of self-esteem (Hall, 1980; Kerwin and Ponterotto, 1995; Stephan, 1992).

Kerwin and Ponterotto's model of biracial (mixed parentage) identity development is based on empirical studies (see Kerwin, Ponterotto, Jackson and Harris, 1993) and incorporates previous research (e.g., Stephan, 1992; Wllliams, 1992) and earlier formulations of biracial identity (e.g., Jacobs, 1992; Kich, 1992; Poston, 1990). Kerwin and Ponterotto's (1995) model provides a useful framework for social work professionals who work with biracial/mixed parentage individuals. Here, their model begins with the Pre-school stage, during which individuals become cognisant of racial and ethnic differences. According to Kerwin and Ponterotto, awareness of racial differences may occur sooner among biracial individuals because of their early experiences with different racial groups. Other biracial children may reach this awareness later if the parents avoid discussion of race and ethnic differences. Entry to school is the next stage in their model. Biracial individuals are likely to be the target of questions raised by other children at this point. During this stage, children begin to use categories in which to place themselves and their families. Kerwin and Ponterotto describe this time as being heavily influenced by the level of integration in the school and the number of role models of differing backgrounds. Pre-adolescence is the next stage and is marked by heightened sensitivity to differences based on physical appearance and other characteristics such as language and culture. Root (1994) describes three primary ways that physical appearance issues at any age manifest for multiracial (mixed parentage) individuals:

1) name seems incongruent with appearance;
2) high level of attention from others due to unique looks; and
3) the ability to modify appearance according to differing situations.

Kerwin and Ponterotto suggest that most biracial individuals will have awareness of the differences between their parents at this stage, but this may not happen for some until an external/environmental factor prompts this realisation. Kerwin and Ponterotto describe the next stage, Adolescence, as a difficult one for biracial individuals because of the external pressure to choose one group over another. This phenomenon is aptly described by Williams (Williams, 1992: 33) as she referred to her own experience of European Americans asking: 'why I do not choose to 'pass' as white, and African American individuals telling her to reject her notion of being biracial 'instead of just admitting I am black'. At this stage, peers are extremely important, and the natural tendency is to conform to social norms in order to be accepted. The norms can and often do include identification with one group, an in-group, and lack of association with other groups. College/Young Adulthood is the next period in Kerwin and Ponterotto's model. They suggest that during this time period identification is still primarily with one culture, but individuals are more likely to reject other's expectations for a singular racial identity and instead move toward appreciation of their multiple heritages. The model ends with Adulthood. During this time individuals continue to integrate the disparate pieces of their own background to form their racial identity. Attainment of this final stage and the accompanying growth-oriented exploratory tendency is predicated on successful resolution of the earlier stages.

Dominelli (2002), notes that 'failure to respond to identity issues adequately is currently exemplified in the work that is being done with children of mixed parentage or heritage' (Dominelli, 2002: 55). It is important for social workers and carers to 'acknowledge the importance of all aspects of ethnicity and their role in promoting a strong sense of self-identity and positive self-image (in mixed parentage children and young people)', (Sinclair and Hai, 2002: 34).

Many researchers stress that it is important for children of mixed parentage to learn to cope as black people or people of colour, because, as noted earlier, white British or American society is ultimately going to categorise them as such (Ladner, 1977; Shackford, 1984; Maxime, 1993). Thus, while mixed parentage children and adolescents may declare themselves as biracial, they must also develop strategies for coping with social resistance or questions about their racial group membership (Root, 1992). In the UK, the Children Act 1989 states that the race, culture, language and religion of children and young people must be addressed in the provision of services. The act: 'also makes it unlawful to ignore the crucial aspects of racial origin and cultural, ethnic, religious and linguistic background of the child in the process of any decision making' (Dwivedi, 2003: 9). In order to meet the need of and help the development of any child, black, white or mixed parentage, it is essential that social workers operate with adequate knowledge, understanding and sensitivity (Robinson, 2001).

Self Examination

In 2001, the Department of Health published the National statistics on the ethnicity of children looked after and on the Child Protection Register. In England, 18 per cent of children in public care are from ethnic minority groups and of these 36 per cent are of mixed heritage. In England, 16 per cent of children on the Child Protection Register were from minority ethnic groups and 35 per cent of this group was of mixed heritage. The increase in the number of mixed parentage children in care poses a new set of challenges for social workers. It will be necessary for social workers to expand their knowledge in this area through continued education, workshops and in-service training. It is also important for social workers to examine their own racial stereotypes and biases as well as their attitudes toward interracial relationships so that they can confront their own prejudices in working with these children and their families.

Social workers need to be aware of their own opinions and biases about interracial marriages, racial identity of biracial persons, and their own personal identity, and be aware of internalised racial and ethnic stereotypes. McRoy and Freeman (1986) found biases of social workers to interracial children reflected in either their overemphasis on children's racial background or their denial that the children's racial heritage had anything to do with the children's behaviour. A firm sense of one's own racial-ethnic identity is especially important for white workers, because whites do not think of themselves as having a racial identity (Wehrly, 1996).

Gibbs (2001), argues that:

> *...the central issue for the clinician [social worker] to assess in evaluating biracial adolescents is their underlying attitudes toward their dual racial/ethnic heritage...Typically, the racially mixed teens seen by clinicians [social workers]*

express ambivalent feelings toward the racial/ethnic backgrounds of both parents, alternatively denigrating and praising the perceived attributes of both groups.

(Gibbs, 2001: 320)

However, he also emphasises that:

Clinicians (social workers) should not assume that psychological or behavioural problems presented by biracial adolescents are necessarily responses to conflicts over their ethnic identity. In fact, clinicians (social workers) must be particularly cautious in inferring a causal relationship between biracial ethnicity and psychosocial maladaptation. Adolescents of all races may experience emotional distress because of normative developmental and social experiences, interpersonal relationships, academic problems, family conflicts, and a host of other causes. In assessing biracial adolescents, clinicians (social workers) must rule out all of these usual stressors before concluding that the adolescents psychological symptoms are the result of ambivalence or rejection of their dual racial heritage.

(Gibbs, 2001: 320)

In a small scale study of children of mixed heritage in need in Islington, Sinclair and Hai (2002) found that: 'the quality of information on children's background needs to be improved; more detail is needed on the specific background of children and their parents and more equally on all aspects of ethnicity-'race', culture, religion and language' (Hai, 2002: 33). Social workers need to ensure that: 'Carers are adequately prepared and supported in helping children develop and sustain a positive self image and to understand their full ethnic background' (Sinclair and Hai, 2002: 33). While the young people in Sinclair and Hai's (2002) study 'generally indicated a positive awareness of their ethnicity, there was still recognition that this did give rise to particular needs around addressing racism, sometimes from within the family, around accepting all aspects of their heritage, especially from an absent parent' (Sinclair and Hai: 34). The authors note that:

Both social workers and carers were active in addressing these needs, for example by trying to maintain some 'quality' contact with the different aspects of the child's background, through engagement with the local 'ethnic' communities...and using of cultural activities to foster positive contact.

(Sinclair and Hai, 2002: 34)

Conclusion

To conclude, demographic trends indicate that there are an increasing number of mixed parentage individuals, and there is a need for continued theory development and empirical research. More research is needed on the role of parents, educators and social workers in helping mixed parentage children develop a healthy sense of identity and in coping with the issues they are likely to face in society.

References

Bagley, C. (1993) *International and Transracial Adoptions*. Aldershot: Avebury.

Banks, N. (1992) Techniques for Direct Identity Work with Black Children. *Adoption and Fostering*, 16: 3, 19–25.

Barn, R. (1990) *Black Children in Local Authority Care: Admission Patterns*. New Community, 16: 2, 229–46.

Barn, R., Sinclair, R. and Ferdinand, D. (1997) *Acting on Principle: An Examination of Race and Ethnicity in Social Services Provision for Children and Families*. London: BAAF.

Bebbington, A. and Miles, J. (1989) The Background of Children who Enter Local Authority Care. *British Journal of Social Work*, 19: 349–68.

Berk, L. (1998) *Development Through the Life Span*. London: Allyn and Bacon.

Berrington, B. (1995) Marriage Patterns and Inter-Ethnic Unions, in Cooleman, D. and Salt, J. (Eds.) *Ethnicity in the 1991 Census*. London: OPCS.

Carter, R.T. (1995) *The Influence of Race and Racial Identity in Psychotherapy: Toward a Racially Inclusive Model*. New York: John Wiley.

Charles, M., Rashid, R. and Thoburn, J. (1992) The Placement of Black Children with Permanent New Families. *Adoption and Fostering*, 16: 3, 13–9.

Cross, W.E. (1978) The Thomas and Cross Models of Psychological Nigrescence: A Literature Review. *The Journal of Black Psychology*, 5: 1, 13–31.

Dominelli, L. (2002) *Anti-oppressive Social Work Theory and Practice*. London: Palgrave/Macmillan.

Dwivedi, K. (Ed.) (2003) *Meeting the Needs of Ethnic Minority Children*. London: Jessica Kingsley.

Erikson, E. (1968) *Identity: Youth and Crisis*. New York: W.W. Norton.

Fatimilehin, I. (1999) Of Jewel Heritage: Racial Socialisation and Racial Identity Attitudes Among Adolescents of Mixed African-Caribbean/White Parentage. *Journal of Adolescence*, 22: 303–18.

Gibbs, J.T. (2001) *Children of Color*. San Francisco, CA: John Wiley and Sons.

Hall, C.C.I. (1980) *The Ethnic Identity of Racially Mixed People: A Study of Black-Japanese*. Unpublished doctoral dissertation, University of California, Los Angeles.

Jacobs, J.H. (1992) Identity Development in Biracial Children, in Root, M.P. (Ed.) *Racially Mixed People in America*. Newbury Park, CA: Sage.

Kerwin, C., Ponterotto, J.G., Jackson, B.L. and Harris, A. (1993) Racial Identity in Biracial Children: A Qualitative Investigation. *Journal of Counseling Psychology*, 40: 221–31.

Kerwin, C. and Ponterotto, J.G. (1995) Biracial Identity Development: Theory and Research, in Ponterotto, J.G., Casas, J.M., Suzuki, L.A. and Alexander, C.M. (Eds.) *Handbook of Multicultural Counseling*. California: Sage.

Kich, G.K. (1992) The Developmental Process of Asserting a Biracial, Bicultural Identity, in Root, M.P. (Ed.) *Racially Mixed People in America*. Newbury Park, CA: Sage.

Ladner, J.A. (1977) *Mixed Families.* Garden City, NY: Anchor/Doubleday.

Marcia, J. (1980) Identity in Adolescence, in Adelson, J. (Ed.) *Handbook of Adolescent Psychology.* New York: Wiley.

Maxime, J. (1993) The Therapeutic Importance of Racial Identity in Working with Black Children who Hate, in Varma, V. (Ed.) *How and Why Children Hate.* London: Jessica Kingsley.

McRoy, R.G. and Freeman, E. (1986) Racial Identity Issues Among Mixed Race Children. *Social Work in Education,* 8: 164–74.

Parham, T. and Helms, J. (1981) The Influence of Black Students' Racial Identity Attitudes on Preference for Counselor's Race. *Journal of Counseling Psychology,* 28: 3, 250–7.

Pinderhughes, E. (1995) Biracial Identity: Asset or Handicap? in Harris, H., Blue, H. and Griffith, E. (Eds.) *Racial and Ethnic Identity.* London: Routledge.

Porterfield, E. (1978) *Black and White Marriages: An Ethnographic Study of Black-White Families.* Chicago: Nelson-Hall.

Poston, W.S.C. (1990) The Biracial Identity Development Model: A Needed Addition. *Journal of Counseling and Development,* 69: 152–5.

Robinson, L. (2001) A Conceptual Framework for Social Work Practice with Black Children and Adolescents in the United Kingdom. *Journal of Social Work,* 1: 2,165–85.

Root, M.P. (1992) *Racially Mixed People in America.* Newbury Park, CA: Sage.

Root, M.P. (1994) Mixed Race Women, in Comas-Diaz, L. and Greene, B. (Eds.) *Women of Color: Integrating Ethnic and Gender Identities in Psychotherapy.* New York: Guilford.

Root, M.P. (Ed.) (1996) *The Multiracial Experience: Racial Borders as the New Frontier.* Thousand Oaks, CA: Sage.

Sebring, D.L. (1985) Considerations in Counselling Interracial Children. *Journal of Non-white Concerns in Personnel and Guidance,* 13: 3–9.

Shackford, K. (1984) Interracial Children: Growing Up Healthy in an Unhealthy Society. *Interracial Books for Children.* 15: 6, 4–6.

Sinclair, R. and Hai, N. (2002) Children of Mixed Heritage in Need in Islington. National Childrens Bureau.

Small, J. (1986) Transracial Placements: Conflicts and Contradictions, in Ahmed, S., Cheetham, J. and Small, J. (Eds.) *Social Work with Black Children and their Families.* London: Batsford.

Stephan, C.W. (1992) Mixed-heritage Individuals: Ethnic Identity and Trait Characteristics, in Root, M.P. (Ed.) *Racially Mixed People in America.* Newbury Park, CA: Sage.

Stonequist, E.V. (1937) *The Marginal Man: A Study in Personality and Culture Conflict.* New York: Russell and Russell.

Tizard, B. and Phoenix, A. (1989) Black Identity and Transracial Adoption, *New Community,* 15: 3, 427–38.

Tizard, B. and Phoenix, A. (1993) *Black, White or Mixed Race: Race and Racism in the Lives of Young People of Mixed Parentage.* London: Allen and Unwin.

Tizard, B. and Phoenix, A. (2002) *Black, White or Mixed Race: Race and Racism in the Lives of Young People of Mixed Parentage.* London: Allen and Unwin.

Wehrly, B. (1996) *Counseling Interracial Individuals and Families.* Alexandria VA: American Counseling Association.

Williams, T.K. (1992) Prism Lives: Identity of Binational Amerasians, in Root, M.P. (Ed.) *Racially Mixed People in America.* Newbury Park, CA: Sage.

Wilson, A. (1987) *Mixed Race Children: A Study of Identity.* London: Allen and Unwin.

Chapter 7

Direct Work with Children of Mixed Parentage

Annabel Goodyer

Introduction

The social work response to mixed race children has a history of using simplistic inter-pretation to deal with situations that can be as complex, varied and sophisticated as the lives of the individual families and children with whom we work.

In this chapter I will explore some of the ways in which theories and paradigms of race and racial issues interact with best practice when working with mixed race families. I have employed the term mixed race as it reflects mainstream cultural concepts of children who have one black parent and one white parent, and who are a group who have yet to define their own identity. Other terminology, such as dual heritage, inter-ethnic, biracial bi-cultural, has not been adopted by me in order to avoid the risk of sounding euphemistic, ambiguous or of being misleading. The general academic discomfort of the use of the term mixed race is seen as reflecting the general discomfort about and lack of resolution of the status of mixed race children within social work academia.

Theoretical Context

Whilst the policies informing social work practice are heavily reliant on underpinning sociological constructs, much of the casework with individuals is more influenced by psychology. This is particularly true of direct work with children and young people, where intervention is more frequently informed by psychoanalytic or behaviourist principles and practices derived from counselling. I would argue that the interpre-tation of the diverse and sometimes complex social situations of service-users from a sociologically constructed binary framework is patronising and at times inappro-priate. Other more subtle theories and findings, such as those of social anthropology (Clarke, 1967; Gellner, 1983; Leinhardt, 1985) can provide a more sophisticated understanding of the complexities of 21st century British culture. As the findings of anthropology are informed by observation and deduction, these theories appear more appropriate to current concepts of social work best practice and are more in line with reflective practice, psycho-analytical thought being more in line with the now out-moded or specialist areas of psycho-social practice.

There are three distinct paradigms of social work theory evident in current perspectives of mixed race children, which are in current use by theorists, academics, commentators and practitioners of social work. Many are based on political and sociological macro perspectives, which may not always be considered to be directly relevant to the individual experiences of service-users and practitioners. The first paradigm is the colour-blind, assimilist view, prevalent in the 1960s and 1970s, which presumed that black and mixed race children could easily be accommodated within existing provisions. The experiences of black and mixed race children within a predominantly white personal social services provision led to a growing awareness of the need for their particular needs to be met within the care system. This coincided with the rise of a defensive stance against racism, a positive black consciousness movement, leading to radical repositioning of social work theory with the anti-discriminatory practice paradigms of the 1980s and 1990s, with the attendant binary perspective of race.

In acknowledging the social construct of race as socially divisive, I do not seek to minimise the dangers faced by mixed race children as a minority group within both black and white cultures. The black radical discourse is acknowledged as an appropriate response to racism encountered within a predominantly white culture. For mixed race children the binary perspective of race has largely resulted in them being identified as black children, because the overriding need they are perceived to have is of learning to cope with, and be protected from, a racist society that sees them as black. That mixed race children can be easily assimilated within black culture is disputed (Okitikpi, 1999b). The emerging paradigm of post-modernist thinking (Katz, 1996) which views racism as a social construct which is itself located in particular settings at particular times, rather than as an inherent part of all experience for black and mixed race people within predominantly white societies, is now gaining ground within social work thinking, if not practice. Within social anthropology Leinhardt (1985) has a model of identity which does not view people as holding fully integrated identities, but as holders of separate identities which are used contextually. Using this analysis a worker may see herself as a feminist when dealing with payroll and employment issues, it is also perfectly possible that she may be a traditionalist in matters of family and adopt a global, 21st Century dress style. In this way it can also be acceptable for mixed race children to generally identify with one ethnic group, but at times or in different contexts with another. Many mixed race children have unique experiences and are capable of adopting identities other than a black identity (Spencer, 1997; Okitikpi, 1999b). Some may choose to have a mono-identity, others may have flexible identities which can adjust to varying social contexts:

> *Such a person (child) may feel biracial at home, white amongst accepting white grandparents and black amongst black relatives, or in an all white classroom.*
>
> (Spencer, 1997: 29)

Spencer's implicit view that being accepted as white is by invitation, but as black is a given, is not necessarily the universal experience of dual heritage children, many of whom report racism from within the black community, where they can perceive themselves, or by others as not quite black, and as part of a despised white society. Although current social work policies hold a perspective of 'a black identity' that can only be properly imparted by a 'black family', this becomes difficult as a concept when working with mixed race families, many of whom appear to raise happy, well-adjusted children who are confident and proud of their dual heritage. There are claims that positive black identity pathologises mixed race identity (Katz, 1996).

Katz's research with mixed race families found that cultural, class and gender identities were interwoven with racial identity. He expressed concern that modern (anti-racist) social work theory has a potential impact on interracial families and mixed race children that marginalises and pathologises them. The children in his study were seen as developing a sense of self in relation to early parenting. The children's later identifications were seen as a response to the social situation in which they found themselves. Those who showed distress he attributed to multiple inter-relating causes, with inter-parental conflict around issues of race, culture, values or personality clashes. Whilst agreeing with much of Katz's analysis, I would argue that other identities such as body image, religion and disability can be integral to children's' concept of self-identity.

Policy

English domestic and family social policy has sought to encompass the increasingly diverse population, with some current policies reflecting more recent concerns surrounding issues of diversity. Current social work policy is moving away from perceiving children as isolated individuals, or members of a nuclear family, to understanding the wider social and environmental contexts within which a child's world is situated. The new framework of assessment, which local authorities in England and Wales are statutorily obliged to use for assessing children in need or at risk, specifically requires social workers to assess extended family, social and neighbourhood networks and community resources. This can be viewed as a move forward from the late 20th century Euro-centric concept of a nuclear family holding sole responsibility for a child, towards an approach which can encompass other perspectives and realities, for example the importance of the maternal grandmother within many Caribbean and African family structures.

It is within the arena of adoption that conflicting perspectives of diversity have been publicly contested. Adoption, with its elements of ownership of children and the supply and demand curves of infants and children considered desirable or acceptable for adoption and couples seeking to adopt healthy babies, is traditionally an emotionally charged area of social work. The ownership of and appropriate parenting of children from black and mixed race families is a hotly contested discourse that received considerable public and media attention during the lengthy legislative process of The Adoption and Children Bill 2002. The adoption policies of local authorities received considerable public criticism, and clauses in the new Act ensure that adoption agencies decisions can now be legally challenged. The placement of children trans-racially or with gay or lesbian parents is no longer for adoption agencies to proscribe. Rather, the wider needs of children for a stable, secure upbringing by a family that they legally belong to being the overriding principle that (should) now guide adoption agencies and their workers. A binary code of adoption matching for adoptive applicants with children can still be considered best practice, but the absence of a suitable racial match should not preclude other adoptive possibilities. Media terminology of 'political correctness' was widely used during the political process of the Adoption Bill to identify same-race placement policies, it generally being viewed as a barrier to the pressing need of children to be placed for adoption or returned to their birth families.

Social inclusion is a policy driver for such measures as the Leaving Care programmes and The Children Leaving Care Act 2000.The obligation on local authorities to provide ongoing care and support to vulnerable young people from the looked after children system may well provide a safety net for mixed race care-leavers who have to contend with enhanced vulnerabilities caused by racism.

Best Practice

Current paradigms of good practice in social work include evidence-based reflective practice, and anti-discriminatory practice. Both are important guiding principles in working with children of mixed parentage, as is an awareness of the impact of racism and the concept of race (Barn, 1999). Acknowledging one's own value-base and being able to put this to one side when working with service-users is a key principle of reflective practice, but somehow when dealing with issues surrounding children and ethnicity prevailing concepts of political correctness or the worker's own issues of racial identity can be seen as more important than the values of the service-user. This marginalisation of service-users perspectives has, I would argue, contributed to the difficulties experienced by mixed race families in their involvement with the personal social services. Prevailing family cultures and key attachments are important components in the understanding of an individual child's identity and socialisation. Placement of children for substitute family care is a hotly contested area concerning issues of ethnic matching (Thoburn, 1988), for example respite care placements with their single heritage siblings would involve considerable dilemmas for the worker to resolve, not least of which is availability of placement choice. By putting the worker's values to one side and offering a service as requested by the families would be one solution (led by reflective practice values), as would placing the children with a family as similar to their own as possible (led by attachment theory). A binary worldview may lead workers to consider splitting the sibling group of the predominantly white family, to place the mixed race child with a black foster-family and the other sibling with a white family. When making such decisions the worker needs to not only balance the tension between the long-term identity needs of the dual heritage child with the immediate need for emotional security, but also to work in partnership with the parent and to facilitate a good working relationship between the parent and foster family. The closest possible replication of the child's main carer within a foster-family will inevitably reduce the separation-anxiety for the child.

I would argue that the identity needs of the mixed race child and the need for the child to acquire the skills for living and succeeding in a predominantly white society are long-term goals which are important to address, but are not necessarily always the most pressing or important issues to be addressed within social work practice with children of mixed parentage.

Social work intervention

Mixed race children and those from ethnic minorities are exposed to the same psychological and social pressures as other children, but additionally have to cope with racism and the dislocation associated with immigration and disrupted family and social networks (Dwivedi, 2002). Where one parent is white/ British, interaction with institutions perceived to have policies and attitudes that undermine the social and family values of ethnic minorities can cause the power balance between the parents to become distorted, a situation which can hamper the effectiveness of social work intervention if un-addressed. These factors can influence the complexity of presenting problems and planned social work interventions.

Family support, child protection and corporate parenting remain the key focus of the services offered to children and families, with therapeutic work being undertaken in each of these areas. An inherent part of therapy is the concept of what is healthy and appropriate, which can be a complex issue to resolve in a diverse society where cultural norms may not be universally held. I would suggest that the concept of what is an appropriate sense of identity for a mixed race child is not undisputed, and particular care needs to be exercised in establishing a perspective that is evidence-based, not merely a reflection of the workers personal stance or prejudice. Good assessment, supervision and regular progress reviews remain the cornerstones of good social work practice in this, as in most areas of social work.

Family Support Work

Family support involves working in partnership with families and acknowledging the families prevailing cultural norms. Within mixed race families, as with other families, the mothers tend to be the dominant family culture. The younger the child, the more dependant the child will be on their prime attachment figure, usually but not invariably the child's natural mother. Children's natural propensity to identify with their main carer (Barn, 1999; Okitikpi, 1999a) should lead a family support worker to presume, until assessment clarifies the situation, that family values and child-rearing practices are those of the mother's cultural background. Prevatt-Goldstein's understanding of mixed race children to be 'black children with a white mother' is informed by research undertaken by Phoenix and Owen (1996) who found 53 per cent of mixed race children to be living with a white mother and black parent, and 45 per cent living with a white single mother, leading her to view mixed race children as 'black children with a white parent'. These figures presume that only two per cent of mixed race children have a black mother and a white father and by deduction that the family culture for most mixed race children will be predominantly white. This has major implications for family support work and for enhancing the parenting of mixed race children, particularly in circumstances where the absence of positive black role models may be an issue.

Family centres are traditionally used by white families, with black families and fathers tending to be under-represented amongst service-users, and this is usually attributed to the dominance of white female staffing, but it may be possible that other factors such as cultural acceptance of a less formal and domestically based service could also contribute to this lower take-up rate. Group involvement in the more social context of the family centre could be inhibiting for mixed race families, who may fear racial intolerance from other families. Workers may need to consider anti-discriminatory practice strategies to combat racism and lack of confidence by families in the likely acceptance and toleration of their cultural norms.

The perceptions that a white mother is unable to fully address the needs of a mixed race child satisfactorily (Ifekwunigwe, 1999) can contribute to undermining the confidence of a parent who may be struggling to cope. A perspective, which is enabling rather than pathologising could contribute to a more positive outcome for workers involved in family support. Acknowledging difference and working in partnership with parents to agree and prioritise tasks, in accordance with the principles of task-centred casework, can be an effective way of working with mixed race families.

Corporate Parenting

The over-representation of mixed race children in the care system is well documented, and there are various speculative assertions advanced to explain the phenomena (Bebbington and Miles, 1989; Okitikpi, 1999a; Tizard and Phoenix, 1993). There appear to be many factors contributing to this situation. Evidence that white mothers of mixed race sons with absent fathers are the group of parents most likely to experience serious parenting difficulties (Katz, 1996), and that they seek to resolve these through social work intervention may not be so surprising. That white British parents may have more confidence in social services agencies is an undisputed premise, as is the assumption that they would be more likely than other parents to seek to resolve parenting difficulties through the intervention of the caring professionals. Practice experience in Inner London has provided me with many experiences of black families who resolve serious parenting problems by sending their children 'back home' (Jamaica, Ghana, Pakistan, Nigeria), where the schools and social mores are perceived to be more disciplined and where extended family networks can offer support. That the parenting of mixed race children where one positive role-model is absent is likely to cause the child difficulty in acquiring a positive sense of identity is central to current thinking (Banks, 1999) and the perceived difficulties of bringing up black children within a predominantly white society may also be contributing to the parenting experiences of the white parents of mixed race children. In summary, there are factors which make the parenting of mixed race children in a predominantly white society more complex and challenging. Those white single parents who lack the resources of family and social networks to sustain them in this task are more likely than other parents to turn to social work agencies for support, leading inevitably to an overrepresentation of mixed race children in the looked-after children population.

Best Practice in corporate parenting, which includes working in partnership with parents, maintaining a sufficient range of placements in order that placement decisions are led by a balancing of the child's needs rather than expediency, careful assessment and regular review to avoid drift, can all minimise the difficulties faced by looked-after children. For mixed race children, poor practice exacerbates the difficulties they may face. The balance between the short-term needs of the child to feel secure within a safe environment that provides continuity of the home culture, must be reviewed promptly to avoid drifting into long-term care with a child forming close attachments to carers who may have difficulty in meeting all the child's long-term needs, particularly their identity needs. Current binary perspectives (Small, 1986; Owusu-Bempah, 1994; Okitikpi, 1999b) which pathologise the placement of mixed race children with white carers, can cause unnecessary emotional distress to children whose placements are decided predominantly by criteria which can marginalise their existent trans-racial attachments.

The current social work discourse concerning the over-representation of mixed race children in the care system (Bebbington and Miles, 1989; Barn, 2002; Okitikpi, 1999a; Tizard and Phoenix, 1993) and the binary classification of all non-white children as black should be issues of serious concern to social work educators, practitioners and service-users. Failure to satisfactorily understand and resolve these issues profoundly affect the admission of children into the care system and also the quality of parenting of mixed race children within the looked after system. Placement decision-making and assessments of appropriate parenting need to be informed by child-led criteria, not political agendas that can be in danger of pathologising otherwise effective parenting on grounds of trans-racial parenting.

Leaving Care

Social inclusion is a policy driver for such measures as the Leaving Care programmes, aimed at decreasing the marginalisation of young people formerly looked after by the local authority. Young people leave care mainly between the ages of 16–18 years, they generally have a lower than average academic achievement (Okitikpi, 1999c) and a higher than average vulnerability to criminal involvement and mental illness. The absence of parental support for some children can be seen to acerbate their vulnerability, as can the absence of a supportive social and family network (Marsh and Peel, 1999). For mixed race children there can be the increased difficulties of managing racism, the lack of a cohesive and ethnically matched readily accessible network and the lack of positive role models to assist in the formation of a positive sense of self.

A history of trans-racial placement can leave care-leavers culturally displaced, with little contact with black or mixed race culture and without the social skills for negotiating relationships within those cultures. The younger the child when admitted to care, the greater the cultural deprivation is likely to be (Ince, 1999). If the care-leaver has a poor self-image, or lack of pride in their dual heritage, they can be particularly vulnerable to negative images held within wider society, without the social and emotional support to redress the balance. The vulnerability of children when leaving care can be increased for mixed race children, with the absence of a host society with whom they can clearly identify.

Child Protection

Issues of child protection are centred on culturally informed, social constructs of child-abuse, with concepts of normal behaviour in a culture pre-determining what is abusive (Smith, et al. 1995). This definition frames social work intervention to protect children as the imposition of generally agreed norms from wider society on a variety of diverse cultural child-rearing practices. It is often differing concepts of discipline that trigger discord within families and between families and the protective services. As with family support, it is likely in most mixed race families that the mother's cultural norms will prevail, for reasons I have outlined in that section. Some of the assessment skills in social work must be pro-actively targeted to accommodate diversity, for example training needs to include information on identifying the signs and symptoms of abuse on different skin types. How many social workers, or medical practitioners, if one reads the Victoria Climbié report carefully, could confidently identify bruising or untreated scabies on a skin colour that differs from their own?

In the Department of Health overview of child protection research (Bullock, 1995) it is claimed that the most important condition for success is the quality of the relationship between a child's family and the professionals involved. A binary perspective, if not shared by the family, can hamper the establishment of an effective working relationship with the professionals, by framing abusive incidents or offering services in a manner which the service-user may perceive as inappropriate or patronising.

Assessment

Essential to current social work practice is a full assessment of individual children's needs including, in instruments such as the framework assessment model, an assessment of cultural and identity needs. The Children Act 1989, UK adoption of the United Nations Convention and subsequent shifts in government policy, have all placed an onus on workers to work in partnership with families and children, and to consult children as to their wishes and feelings on major decisions made by others on their behalf. Good communication skills are needed to establish the child's perspective and views, if one is to avoid the danger of ascribing needs, rather than understanding or interpreting the child's needs.

Looking at the needs of individual children within their social context of family, neighbourhood and community is required when using the statutory framework assessment procedures. This instrument of assessment is helpful when assessing the needs of mixed race children, particularly if the other members of the child's household are mono-racial. The existence or absence of appropriate role models, positive opportunities for cultural information and expression, opportunities for appropriate personal care (skin and hair care), and culturally appropriate literature should be addressed in the Framework Assessments.

Mixed race children who have a negative self-image or who attempt to deny parts of their racial make-up need to be identified. Without accurate assessment and a fully resourced plan to remedy any shortcomings in the child's social environment, this problem could become potentially dangerous to the child's emerging personality. An ongoing lack of provision of a suitable range of placements is not an acceptable reason to place a child trans-racially, but for a mixed race child I would consider a placement where the main carer is of the same race and culture as the child's main attachment figure, usually the birth mother, would be a racially suitable match. Ideally the presence in the household of an adult who is of the same race, gender and culture as the child's other birth parent would make the placement a good match in terms of racial issues.

My own practice experience of working with a mixed race adolescent boy, Michael, returning from a long-term black foster family to live with his white grandmother, was that it was contact with a dual-heritage visiting uncle which he found most helpful in resolving his identity issues and dilemmas. Practical skills such as hair and clothing styles deemed suitable for encountering potential employers, police and the courts and the transformation when clubbing and socialising with black peers were part of the role modelling that occurred spontaneously within their relationship. Whilst this may have caused me unease on occasions as to whether or not Michael was denying his black identity, Michael and his uncle perceived these social skills as a vital and effective part of knowing your way around the system.

Identity

Many workers feel daunted at the prospect of ever managing to conceptualise such a nebulous concept as identity and culture, let alone establish what an individual child may need, but I would argue that with patience and reasonable technical and deductive skills, establishing these needs is within the expertise of most social workers. Children with learning or sensory impairment may benefit from joint working with specialists, for example Makaton skills are required to ease communication with some children. Carers, teachers and those who deal with a child on a daily basis are often those most able to give advice on requisite communication skills, even if they may not be the most appropriate co-workers when tackling confidential matters.

Post-modern anti-racists (Katz, 1996; Gilroy, 1987; Okitikpi, 1999b) maintain that race, culture, class and gender are all part of complex social phenomena, from which particular forms of racism originate. These forms of racism are local and context bound, suggesting in my view that anti-racist strategies and the skills to deal with racism need to be taught within a social or family context in order to be successfully local and context bound. Mainstream British society and current social policies may choose to categorise service-users by perceived ethnicity but the concept of racial identity being the predominant component of one's identity may not be one shared by all service-users, and many families believe their religious or national identity is of equal or greater significance (Gellner, 1983).

The opportunity to form positive, ongoing relationships with black, white and mixed race positive role models can greatly assist a mixed race child to obtain a balanced and positive self identity. That these relationships can only be formed with current or future carers is a social work myth, and at various times in a child's life, other placement priorities may take precedence, for example to remain in the same school neighbourhood. The provision of positive white role models and a valuing of their white heritage are commonly available within mainstream British society for mixed race children, but the validation of black culture and identity may need to be actively sought.

Indicators that should alert a worker to a child's sense of self and relationship with others needing direct intervention by professionals include self-harm, aggressive behaviour and depression (Prevatt-Goldstein, 1999).

Communication Skills

Establishing a safe, trusting space, where a child can openly discuss issues or confide matters of concern, is the initial priority in communicating effectively with children, and boundaried discourse is generally experienced as the most appropriate. Thanking the child for agreeing to see you, followed by an open question about the child's understanding of the interview is a well-established interview technique. A statement about the purpose of your involvement can establish the initial boundary, followed up with an explanation of how you will deal with the information received. An opportunity to ask questions can also offer reassurance about the many anxieties or concerns the child may have about you and your involvement in their life. Following the usual best practice concepts of putting the child at ease first through conversation on general issues can be an initial stumbling block for workers who are not in current contact with a particular age or cultural group, with incorrectly applied terminology being distinctly uncool. With very young children an ice-breaking proffering of a toy can be of great assistance, for example I have found felt-tip pens which smell are useful, the red pen smelling of strawberries has proved to intrigue several seemingly aloof children.

Moving an interview from general to specific topics is a matter of individual skill, but the visual indicators from a child's body language can be an indicator that the child has begun to relax in your company. Body language is an important part of communication, and most of us can be intimidated by another person who is twice our size standing over us, whilst sitting down and adopting an open stance are clear indicators of a willingness to be approached, as are a smile and neutral voice tones. Choice of vocabulary is also important, and although at times of stress most social workers have an urge to retreat into jargon, using long words when a small word will do is not a good method for communicating with a child. Walking a tightrope between being readily understood without being patronising can be a difficult knack, but in my experience children can be rather generous about giving feedback on this issue.

Establishing a comfortable environment for the child to explore their own sense of racial identity, whilst also offering a positive validation and respect for both racial aspects of the child's identity remains one of the key communication tasks in working with mixed race children. Once a comfortable discourse has been established, the child can return to these areas, when he or she has issues they need to resolve.

Direct Work

There are a range of methods that can be used in working directly with children, with care taken to select a method that reflects children's individual competencies and interests. Paper working and methods that avoid direct eye contact can be more comfortable and less challenging for many children. Banks (1992; 1999) recommends offering a limited palette of coloured crayons and asking children to draw themselves, as a means of introducing the topic of race. Mirror work, where you ask the child to look in a mirror and describe what they see can be used most effectively in situations where the worker is of the same ethnic origin as the child, or has a confident, affirming, comfortable and established discourse with the child about difference. More complex methods that involve mapping children's family and social networks can also work well, with children enjoying one-to-one attention. It is the discussions that these methods engender that provide the diagnostic or therapeutic material for workers, with skill, empathy and sensitivity being demonstrated to convey positive affirmation of both aspects of the racial origins of a mixed race child. In order to avoid the ascription of cultural identity to a particular child, an awareness of one's own values is a pre-requisite. If the worker has a binary perspective, perceiving all dual-heritage children as being required to self-identify with a black community, this must be identified as a personal perspective and not used to pathologise children who do not have a similar value. As Okitikpi, 1999a; Barn, 1999 and many others claim, children may have a range of perspectives on their cultural position, with infants having a propensity to identify with their main carer.

Middle childhood can be expected to be a time when children gain a growing realisation about themselves as a family member, and as a member of their community. Adolescence will provide a greater challenge to all children, with experimentation and an emerging awareness of where they hope to fit into a wider society being part of the usual experience for westernised young people.

Self-identity is not a fixed concept for most children, and this fluidity can be viewed as a normal part of growing up. 'Tell me about your school friends?' can be a useful question to ascertain a child's level of racial consciousness, with follow up questions about such issues as 'Do children at your school go around in gangs?' 'How do they choose which gang to go around in'? What happens when you are angry with your friends?' 'What names do you call them when they've really upset you?' 'What do they call you?' 'What does that mean, I have not come across that word before?' is a better admission of your ignorance, than risking ascribing an incorrect meaning. Children are used to a world where lots of participants do not fully understand what is happening around them and are usually rather generous with explanations. Implicit in understanding a child's perspective is gaining a concept of their world, with the subject child being your main informant. You may well choose to check this with other perspectives, from carers, professionals and records, at a later stage, but the expert in this area is almost certainly the children themselves.

Areas where social workers might usefully enable dual heritage children to have their needs met include: enabling the formation of a positive self identity or identities; having an understanding and respect for both aspects of their cultural and ethnic heritages; acquiring the skills needed to succeed in a predominantly white society, including the skills to combat racism and acquiring the skills to form positive relationships within their birth family, extended families, peer groups and communities.

Whilst I do not agree with Alleyne's claim that 'white children's needs are acknowledged and well catered for in every aspect of society', and that 'identity needs of black children are not recognised, let alone responded to' (Alleyne, 1987: 7) it is probable that within mainstream British culture the recognition and enhancement of a positive black identity for mixed race children may be more difficult to achieve than for the enhancement of aspects of their white identity.

Enhancing a positive black identity for the child need not necessarily be difficult for white social workers to achieve, but it may be more appropriate, at times, for a black or mixed race worker to tackle at least some of this task. Demonstrating an awareness, respect and positive attitude towards the child's black heritage is within the practice requirements of any children and families worker acting as a 'good enough' corporate parent, as is highlighting the achievements of black and dual heritage people and ensuring the provision of appropriate resources, for example books, cards and toys depicting black people. Providing cultural, recreational or leisure activities that are led by black or dual heritage adults can also be a method of enhancing a positive black identity formation. Banks (2002), advocates that a positive identity is socially viable and psychologically satisfying, not an arrogant, elitist one, but one where 'children display strong ethnic group worth without being dismissive of other cultural groups'. The presence of positive role models from both racial groups and the ability of the adults to openly discuss issues of difference are perceived by him to facilitate the formation of such an identity.

Life-story work

Life story work is now valued within social work as a favoured medium for direct work with children. As with other forms of direct work, an awareness of one's own values and avoiding the ascription of cultural identity to a child are important starting points. As I mentioned previously, if the worker has a binary perspective, perceiving all dual-heritage children as being required to self-identify with a black community, this must be identified as a personal perspective and not used to pathologise children who do not share this worldview. It is important to acknowledge that the inherent concept of co-authoring a child's personal history gives the worker considerable responsibility in the appropriate interpretation and selection of relevant material. The nature of the power imbalance in the relationship between child and worker can exaggerate the impact of the workers perspective of the situation. Careful preparation and attention to listening to the child's views is the key to successful life story work. Photographs of family members, including absent relations can be an excellent way of introducing the concept of racial and ethnic difference. Retaining a neutral stance and allowing the child's understanding of difference to unfold is usually effective, with reassurance given, if needed. Within mainstream white-dominated British society it is likely that a mixed race child will have absorbed the prevailing social norms of placing a high value on their white heritage, but being prepared to offer examples of important black role models and acquiring social competence in the child's particular cultural heritage are ways the worker can assist in addressing unmet needs. Whether the direct work is therapeutic in design, or intended as a way of presenting the child's personal history in an accessible form, the process of the work itself can often be experienced by the child as both. For some children difference is a highly emotive issue, which if dealt with in a comfortable, safe emotional environment can allow a child to explore the issue and find a language to share concerns. These are unlikely to be the same issues that concern the worker. Asking children to draw pictures of themselves and their families, with an array of different coloured crayons available can be a good starting point.

Adolescence

Dual-heritage adolescents, in common with other adolescents, may seek to experiment with various identities. A worker's theoretical stance that seeks to pathologise some or any of these choices as unhealthy or inappropriate is denying the children the opportunity of experimentation, which is generally viewed as a 'normal' stage of development. Dual-heritage children may have a wider range of models for self-expression to choose from than other adolescents, and exploring part of a culture does not necessarily imply any sinister ambition to deny the rest of one's heritage, in the long-term. The richness of a dual heritage can be perceived as a cause for celebration. A chosen mode of self-expression can be located in rebellious, aspirational, peer group, fashionable, traditional, musical or many other influences. The complexities of adolescent culture are probably beyond the knowledge base of most of us, but adolescents generally can respond to perceived genuine interest with very long explanations.

Conclusion

The socialisation of mixed race children is undoubtedly complex, with the presence of appropriate positive role models from both parental backgrounds and an ability of the carers to openly discuss issues of difference having an impact on the children's ability to form a positive racial identity. Children who learn to successfully engage with both cultural groups can be perceived to have an enriched social experience. For children whose circumstances do not provide the presence of appropriate positive role models from both parental backgrounds and who have carers unable to openly discuss issues of difference, there is a particular danger of the child forming a negative sense of self or of being ill-equipped to encounter racism. Whilst the black radical social work movement has contributed greatly to improving standards of care for black and dual heritage children, it may be the time to move to a less fundamentalist stance, where the complexities of the individual child's experiences and heritage are seen in a more sophisticated manner than that of a binary world view. I am not, however, advocating a return to the earlier social work paradigms of colour-blindness, when black and dual heritage children suffered from racism, ignorance and a lack of suitable role models.

For mixed race families, and in particular for mixed race children, it can be difficult to negotiate social situations and for children's needs to be successfully accommodated within contexts where a binary perspective of race is in operation. Best practice can minimise but not eradicate the difficulties for mixed race families.

References

Alleyne, J. (1987) *Issues in the Development of a Positive Black Identity.* London: Black Child Care Series.

Banks, N. (1992) Techniques for Direct Identity Work with Black Children. *Adoption and Fostering* 16: 3, 19–25.

Banks, N. (2002) Mixed race Children and Families, in Dweivedi, K. *Meeting the Needs of Ethnic Minority Children.* London: Jessica Kingsley.

Barn, R. (1999) *Working with Black Children and Adolescents in Need.* London: BAAF.

Bebbington, A. and Miles, J. (1989) *The Background of Children Who Enter Local Authority Care.* London. BAAF.

Bullock, R. et al. (1995) *Child Protection: Messages from Research.* London: HMSO.

Clarke, E. (1957) *My Mother who Fathered Me: A Study of the Family in Three Selected Communities in Jamaica.* London: Allen and Unwin.

Deann, C. (2002) *The Arguments for and Against Trans-racial Placements.* East Anglia: UEA Social Work Monographs.

Dwivedi, K. (2002) *Meeting the Needs of Ethnic Minority Children.* London: Jessica Kingsley.

Gellner, E. (1983) *Nations and Nationalism.* Oxford: Blackwell.

Gilroy, P. (1987) *There ain't no Black in the Union Jack.* London: Routledge.

Ifekwunigwe, J. (1999) *Scattered Belongings: Cultural Paradoxes of 'Race', Nation and Gender.* London: Routledge.

Ince, L. (1999) Preparing Black Young People for Leaving Care, in Barn, R. (Ed.) *Working with Black Children and Adolescents in Care.* London: BAAF.

Katz, I. (1996) *The Construction of Racial Identity in Children of Mixed Parentage.* London: Jessica Kingsley.

Leinhardt, G. (1985) Self, Public and Private, in Carruthers, M. (1985) *The Category of the Person.* Cambridge: CUP.

Mallows, M. (1989) Abercave Weekend: Exploring the Needs of Inter-racially Adopted Young People. *Adoption and Fostering,* 13: 3.

Marsh, P. and Peel, M. (1999) *Leaving Care in Partnership – Family Involvement with Care Leavers.* London, Stationery Office.

Okitikpi, T. (1999a) Why are There Such a High Percentage of Mixed Race Children in Care? *Child Care in Practice. Northern Ireland Journal of Multi-disciplinary Child Care Practice,* 5: 4. Oct.

Okitikpi, T. (1999b) Identification of Mixed Race Children. *Issues in Social Work Education,* 19: 1, 93–106.

Okitikpi, T. (1999c) Educational Needs of Black Children in the Care System, in Barn, R. (Ed.) *Working with Black Children and Adolescents in Need.* London: BAAF.

Owusu-Bempah, K. (1994) Race, Self-identity and Social Work. *British Journal of Social Work,* 24: 123–36.

Phoenix, A. and Owen, C. (1996) From Miscegenation to Hybridity: Mixed Relationships and Mixed Parentage in Profile, in Bernstein, B. and Brannen, J. (Eds), *Children, Research and Policy.* 111–35. London, Taylor and Francis.

Prevatt-Goldstein, B. (1999) Direct Work with Black Children with a White Parent, in Barn, R. (Ed.) *Working with Black Children and Adolescents in Need.* London: BAAF.

Small, J. (1986) Trans-racial Placements: Conflicts and Contradictions, in Ahmed, S. et al. (Eds.) *Social Work with Black Children and their Families.* London: BAAF.

Smith, M. et al. (Eds.) (1995) cited in Bullock, R. et al. (Eds.) *Child Protection: Messages from Research.* London: HMSO.

Spencer, J.M. (1997) *The New Coloured People: The Mixed Parentage People in America.* New York: University Press.

DoH (2002) *The Adoption and Children Bill 2002.* London: Stationery Office.

DoH (2000) *The Children Leaving Care Act 2000.* London: Stationery Office.

DoH (1989) *The Children Act 1989.* London: Stationery Office.

Tizard, B. and Phoenix, A. (1989) Black Identity and Transracial Adoptions, *New Community,*15: 3, 427–37.

Tizard, B. and Phoenix, A. (1993) *Black, White or Mixed race.* London: Routledge.

Thoburn, J. (1988) *Child Placement: Principles and Practice.* Community Care Practice Handbooks, Aldershot: Wildwood House.

Chapter 8

Exploring the Discourse Concerning White Mothers of Mixed Parentage Children

Vicki Harman and Ravinder Barn

Introduction

This chapter builds upon earlier research by one of the authors which has documented the high number of mixed parentage children in the public care system, and highlighted the social and economic circumstances of lone white mothers (Barn, 1993; Barn et al., 1997; Barn, 1999). There are currently 4,700 children of mixed parentage (8 per cent of the in-care population) in the care system in England (DfES, 2004). The most common family type that these children come from prior to entry into care has been shown to be a lone parent family. By combining the findings of two previous studies involving mixed parentage children Barn (1999) showed that the majority of children had lived with their white birth mother before entering care.

The rationale behind exploring the circumstances of this type of family is not simply rooted in family structure demographics. Mothers are considered to play a key role in the socialisation of their children and are recognised as transmitters of culture (Ribbens, 1994). Thus, the identity development of mixed parentage children whose ethnicity has become the subject of much debate and discussion is considered, by some, to be a source of concern.

This chapter focuses on two key aspects of this discourse, where attention has been particularly focused on white mothers' ability to:

- Equip children to deal with racism.
- Provide a positive racial identity.

Following this, we will consider parental strategies for positive identity development. The discussion in this chapter is located in the context of the mothers' experiences, as gleaned from existing qualitative accounts, which offer an insight into some of the problems and challenges the mothers face. The issues raised relate to both partnered and lone mothers, however, some experiences may bear down particularly hard on mothers in families where the black partner is absent.

Equipping children to deal with racism

Research evidence has shown that mixed parentage children are likely to experience racism, for example, in the school playground (Tizard and Phoenix, 1993; Barter, 1999; Alibhai-Brown, 2001; Cline et al., 2002; Ali, 2003). Significantly, they are likely to experience name-calling not only from white but also from black people (Tizard and Phoenix, 1993; Alibhai-Brown, 2001). Tizard and Phoenix (1993) found that 72 per cent of their sample of 58 young people had been called racist names, and for 22 per cent this had been a frequent experience. In light of such experiences, mothers often have the role of comforting children, and helping them to develop strategies to be able to deal with racism and the pain it causes. Some more politically aware mothers may also seek to depersonalise racism by helping children to understand the historical and societal context of racism (Twine, 2003). There have been calls for social worker practitioners to listen to these experiences and understand the strain that racism places on children and their families (Prevatt-Goldstein, 1999). In a report by the 'Early Years Trainers Anti-Racist Network' a white mother describes her family's experience:

> *My daughter is six years old and for the last two years she has been consciously tackling racism. I cannot express how sick this makes me feel, that children so young have to struggle, they have to grow up quick and be twice as good as the white children next to them.*

> (EYTARN, 1995: 3)

Research has shown that being involved in mixed relationships and having mixed parentage children can make some white women more conscious of racism and their own position of whiteness (Frankenberg, 1993; Verbian, 2003). However, some writers, such as Jane Ifekwunigwe, have questioned the extent to which white mothers can fully appreciate the situation of their children:

> *...despite their best intentions, sometimes white mothers do not completely understand the extent to which their own white privilege separates them from the 'everyday racism' (Essed, 1991) which their black daughters face.*

> (Ifekwunigwe, 1999: 172)

This suggests that a full appreciation of racism is not possible for white mothers. This is because they 'have not walked in that child's shoes'; (Camper, 1994: 6). Frankenberg suggests that white women's experience of an altered position in the 'racial order' was 'albeit on contingent and provisional terms' (1993: 135). This impermanence is illustrated in the following quote of a lone mother living on a South London council estate:

> *It is terrible to say this because I am talking about my own children and I love them. But because I am white, if I am alone, I can walk anywhere. I feel free. Nobody bothers. But when the children are with me, I am a prisoner to what people feel*

about me and the children. And you do want to belong to your own kind. It hurts. It's like that film where you wake up one day and you are black.

(Alibhai-Brown, 2001: 122)

This quote suggests that the mother has perceived a sudden change in her social position as a result of having mixed parentage children. Nick Banks (1996) argues that racism, directed both at themselves and their children, presents one of the many experiences which white mothers face, for which their past experiences may not have fully prepared them. It is therefore important to consider the supportive networks that may help mothers to cope with such new experiences and minimise their effects on children (Harman, forthcoming).

Racism from within the family

Mothers and children may not only be facing racism from 'outsiders' but also from within their own families (Tizard and Phoenix, 1993; Barter, 1999). France Winddance Twine's 1999 study involving 65 white mothers of mixed parentage children living in London and the East Midlands, found that racist attitudes were extremely common amongst grandparents. These attitudes were demonstrated in a variety of ways including using racist language, declining to mention and avoiding contact with their grandchildren, and withholding physical affection. This was illustrated in the account of Erica, a twenty-nine year-old mother with three young children:

I don't think [my father] still can believe that he has family that are black, you know. It's very offensive and hurtful to him, I think. Because my sister had a baby last year and he will make a fuss of her – of my sister's little girl. And I suppose in a way that's quite hurtful [to me] really – that he'll make a fuss of her baby and to my children he's not so loving.

(Twine, 1999)

This study illustrates that many mothers are operating a difficult balancing act, on one hand not being able to relinquish contact with their immediate family (the very people whom they may be relying on for support), and on the other seeking to protect their children and their children's self-esteem from their racist attitudes. This was found to be extremely stressful for mothers, leading to nervous collapse or clinical depression in severe cases (Twine, 1999).

A further dimension to this task of equipping children to deal with racism is that some mothers may be confronting their own prejudices. Barn (1993) showed that the majority of white mothers of mixed parentage children in the care system were the sole carer prior to the child's entry into care. Black fathers were very rarely in the picture. In these lone parent family situations, there is further socio-economic disadvantage. In caring for their children alone, some white mothers, understandably, feel abandoned by the black fathers. While some mothers were able to rationalise their situation as a 'normal relationship breakdown', others expressed anger and hurt, which manifested itself in racially prejudiced terms. Negative views about the black partner were sometimes transmitted to the children, where mothers consciously or unconsciously held a low opinion of their children. Banks (1992) has similarly documented the process by which negative, angry feelings towards the black ex-partner can become racialised and transferred onto children. This is demonstrated in the following comments of a mother with an eight-year-old son:

> *Every time I look at him (the child) he reminds me of that black bastard and what he did to me. If Nathan ever grows up to be like him I'll kill him.*

> (Banks, 1992: 33)

Research has documented how arguments in interracial relationships can become racialised, even when at first they appear to have nothing to do with race (Frankenberg, 1993; Alibhai-Brown, 2001). Thus, racial tension in the external world creeps into personal relationships (Frankenberg, 1993). Clearly this process has worrying consequences when it occurs in the context of parent-child relationships.

The psychoanalytic model has been used to understand the attitude and feelings of white mothers towards their mixed parentage children. Here, white mothers are perceived to be inherently racist as a result of their early childhood experiences. In his critical comment on the writings of Henriques (1974) and Holland and Holland (1984), Katz (1996) argues that white women's relationships with black men are viewed as a consequence of early experiences with their fathers:

> *In this view, the mothers' low self-esteem is caused by poor bonding with their fathers and themselves. They feel unworthy of white men like their idealised father, and the relationship with the black man symbolises their anger with their fathers and themselves. Children are a concrete symbol of this anger and ambivalence, and so the anger towards the black partner is projected on the children.*

> (Katz, 1996: 196)

With reference to this model, Katz warns of the danger of pathologising, whereby mothers are seen as child-like victims who damage their own children. Such a model fails to give adequate weight to the 'multiplicity of risk factors' including material hardship and a lack of supportive networks' (Barn, 1999: 283), which often become part of the lived experience of families in need. Similarly, caution must be exercised in the application of the more worrying findings of clinical studies such as Banks (1992), which are clearly based on small numbers, in a therapeutic setting, and therefore cannot be considered to be representative of mothers of mixed parentage children in general. There remains the need for a more thorough understanding of the circumstances and experiences of white mothers, both those receiving support from social services and those in the community (Barn, 1999). This chapter now moves on to explore the second aspect of the discourse concerning white mothers, which is that of racial identity.

Providing a positive racial identity

Over the last two decades, the field of social work has come to recognise the pernicious effects of racism in the lives of children, and the importance of a positive racial or ethnic identity. The early practical books of the black psychologist, Jocelyn Maximé are a good example of these developments (Maximé, 1987; 1991 and 1994).

However, there is not a consensus over what constitutes a positive identity for a mixed parentage child. A number of commentators have argued that a black identity is the only positive identity, due to the realities of racism in society and the fact that irrespective of how the young person may view themselves, society will view them black (Robinson, 1995; Richards, 1995; Prevatt-Goldstein, 1999; Banks, 2002). Power differentials and racism in society means that a child may develop a poor view of the black dimension of their identity, and may internalise racism, possibly even leading to self-hatred. (Maximé, 1987). Therefore, the child must be encouraged to adopt an identity that is comfortable with blackness. Otherwise they may experience hurt and rejection when trying to fit into white society, with damaging psychological effects.

On the other hand, others have argued that mixed parentage children belong to both black and white groups, and should not be encouraged to focus exclusively on their black heritage (Tizard and Phoenix, 1993; Okitikpi, 2001, 2002). It has been argued that: 'prescriptions for healthy identities should not be decreed by experts' (Katz, 1996: 194).

In their 1993 study of mixed parentage young people, Tizard and Phoenix defined a positive racial identity as '…all those young people who said both that they felt pleased and proud of their mixed parentage, and that, even if in the past they had wanted to be another colour, they no longer did so'; (Tizard and Phoenix, 1993: 59). Conversely, a problematic identity was defined as, '…those who said they would still rather be another colour, and/or those whose spontaneous comments indicated that they were unhappy with, or confused about, their mixed parentage'; (Tizard and Phoenix, 1993: 59). An intermediate identity is also suggested by the authors in which a person neither wishes to be another colour, or exhibits positive feelings about their racial identity. In a non-clinical sample of 58 mixed parentage (black/white), adolescents, predominantly from middle-class two parent families in London, 60 per cent of the sample were reported to have a positive racial identity, 20 per cent had a problematic identity, and 20 per cent had an intermediate identity (Tizard and Phoenix, 1993). Those with a problematic identity were more likely to be affiliated to white people. The findings also pointed to the situational, fluid, changing nature of racial identity (Tizard and Phoenix, 1993). Many young people defined themselves differently according to the situation and who they were with; this was not associated with identity confusion (ibid).

Most non-clinical studies have shown the racial or ethnic identity of mixed-parentage young people to be generally positive and unproblematic (Tizard and Phoenix, 1993; Gibbs and Hines, 1992; Fatimilehin, 1999). However, there is evidence to show that the 'desire to be white' is not uncommon in clinical and non-clinical samples (Banks, 1992; Maximé, 1993; Tizard and Phoenix, 1993). In the Tizard and Phoenix study, over half of the sample had wished to be another colour in the past, and the vast majority of these had expressed a desire to be white. Abuse from peers, and the uncomfortable feelings of difference had contributed to children's desire to be white, and fit in. Studies have not found a straightforward relationship between living with a lone parent and racial identity (Frankenberg, 1993; Ali, 2003). The significance of living in a multiracial area, and the input by parents and significant others have been identified as vital factors (Tizard and Phoenix, 1993; Rosenblatt, Karis and Powell, 1995). This chapter now moves on to consider parental input in more detail.

Parental strategies for positive identity development

From her interviews with 65 white mothers in the East Midlands and London, Twine (2003) documents a range of approaches employed by mothers, such as alternative history lessons, promoting black culture through decorations and pictures in the home, books, toys and music. Some mothers employed a comprehensive range of strategies to provide children with a positive black identity. The emphasis on the 'minority' culture helped to offset concern that the child was surrounded by white culture all the time, and therefore may internalise a negative view of black people. Some mothers chose to cook particular food to help promote an appreciation of the minority culture. Another study found that mothers' strategies include joining peer support groups, reinforcing black culture, discussion on racial issues and choosing where to live, and warning their children about societal hostility (O'Donoghue, 2000).

Support networks of friends and family (on both sides) can help to promote positive identity development. Contemporary studies of family support have pointed to the importance of informal supportive networks for families (Gardner, 2003). Yet white mothers are often constrained by negative social perceptions (stigma and social disapproval) and structural forces (financial hardship, geographical location) which mean that they frequently do not have the kinds of supportive networks of friends and family that would be ideal. Lone mothers, without the emotional and financial support of a partner, may be particularly vulnerable to such difficulties. Banks supports this with his findings that many women felt isolated and had become separated from their previous friends and family as a result of 'crossing of rigid racial social boundaries'; (Banks, 1996: 21). Wilson (1987) argued that those mothers who were most successful in promoting positive identity development were those who were involved in a black or mixed community. Interviews with white mothers have suggested some value having black friends who can act as 'positive role models' for their children (Tizard and Phoenix, 1993). A more recent study found that lone white mothers particularly pointed to the importance of their children being around black people (Ali, 2003). Mothers in mixed parentage families are frequently active in seeking, creating and strengthening those networks that they feel will benefit their parenting (Harman, forthcoming). This may include strong friendships with black people who can assist their children with feeling positive about their racial heritage. However, contact with the black community and black organisations may be both supportive and challenging for white mothers (Twine, 2003). Parental peer support groups and organisations may also be a useful source of support and information for some parents.

We have devised the following model to demonstrate key strategies that parents have been found to employ. Strategies include living in a multiracial area, utilising supportive networks of peers, family and friends, multi-cultural books, toys and events and discussion of racial and cultural issues. Evidence suggests that many mothers use a range of such strategies to deal with racial hostility, and to promote a positive upbringing for their children. However, others may view such strategies as irrelevant or undesirable, and fear that they could make the child feel 'different' or put too much emphasis on the 'black side' of their heritage at the expense of the 'white side'. Such differing standpoints reflect mothers' views about race relations in Britain

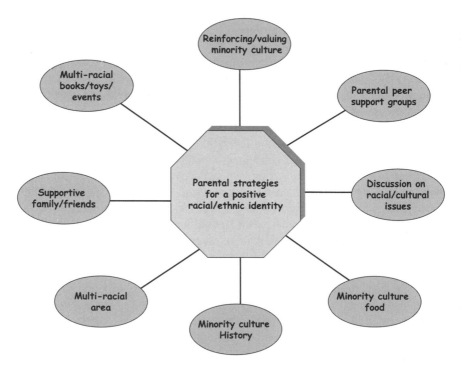

Figure 1: A model of parental strategies for positive racial and ethnic identity development in children and young people of mixed parentage

and the politics of identity. More research is needed into the diversity of strategies employed by mothers and the potential influence these have on the identity development of mixed parentage children.

Conclusion

This chapter has pointed to the way in which white mothers continue to receive considerable attention about their ability to care for mixed parentage children, particularly in the areas of dealing with racism and nurturing a positive identity. It is evident that many mothers cope with very difficult situations. However, for others, the difficulties are insurmountable, which may help to explain the high number of children from this background facing exclusion or using crisis services. Particular stress factors include social isolation, financial difficulties, poor housing, experience of racism, and lack of support.

This chapter has suggested that some of the difficulties may be exacerbated where the family structure is lone parent. For some mothers in mixed parentage families, the father represents a potential (yet absent) link to the black community, knowledge of black culture, and coping strategies for dealing with racism. This chapter has also pointed to the range of strategies mothers can adopt to help promote positive racial identity development.

There is the need for a sensitive and non-pathologising exploration of lone mothers' circumstances and the issues that affect them. Such research will help agencies provide relevant and useful services to mixed families who (as the care statistics tell us) are having difficulty coping.

References

Ali, S. (2003) *Mixed Race, Post-Race: Gender, New Ethnicities and Cultural Practices.* Oxford and New York: Berg.

Alibhai-Brown, Y. and Montague, A. (1992) *The Colour of Love: Mixed Race Relationships.* London: Virago.

Alibhai-Brown, Y. (2001) *Mixed Feelings: The Complex Lives of Mixed Race Britons.* London: The Women's Press.

Banks, N. (1992) Some Considerations for 'Racial' Identification and Self Esteem when Working with Mixed Ethnicity Children and their Mothers as Social Services Clients. *Social Services Research,* 3, 32–41.

Banks, N. (1996) Young Single White Mothers with Black Children in Therapy. *Clinical Child Psychology and Psychiatry,* 1: 1, 19–28 London, Sage Publications.

Banks, N. (2002) What is a Positive Black Identity? in Dwivedi, K. (Ed.) *Meeting the Needs of Ethnic Minority Children Including Refugee, Black and Mixed Parentage Children.* London and New York: Jessica Kingsley.

Barn, R. (1993) *Black Children in the Public Care System.* London: Batsford.

Barn, R., Sinclair, R. and Ferdinand, D. (1997) *Acting on Principle: An Examination of Race and Ethnicity in Social Services Provision for Children and Families.* London: BAAF.

Barn, R. (1999) White Mothers, Mixed-parentage Children and Child Welfare. *British Journal of Social Work,* 29: 2, 269–84.

Barter, C. (1999) *Protecting Children from Racism and Racial Abuse: A Research Review.* London: NSPCC.

Camper, C. (Ed.) (1994) *Miscegenation Blues: Voices of Mixed Race Women.* Toronto: Sister Vision.

Cline, T., Abreu, G., Fihosy, C., Gray, H., Lambert, H. and Neale, J. (2002) Children Who Have a Mixed Heritage Background, in *Minority Ethnic Pupils in Mainly White Schools.* University of London Research Report.

Department for Education and Skills (2004) *Children Looked After by Local Authorities, Year Ending 31 March 2003, England.* London: DfES.

Early Years Trainers Anti-Racist Network (1995) *The Best of Both Worlds…Celebrating Mixed Parentage.* Wallasey: EYTARN.

Essed, P. (1991) *Understanding Everyday Racism: An Interdisciplinary Theory.* London, Sage.

Fatimilehin, I. (1999) Of Jewel Heritage: Racial Socialization and Racial Identity Attitudes Amongst Adolescents of Mixed Afro-Caribbean/White Parentage. *Journal of Adolescence,* 22: 303–18.

Frankenberg, R. (1993) *The Social Construction of Whiteness: White Women, Race Matters.* London: Routledge.

Gardner, R. (2003) *Supporting Families: Child Protection in the Community.* Chichester: Wiley.

Gibbs, J.T. and Hines, A.M. (1992) Negotiating Ethnic Identity: Issues for Black-White Biracial Adolescents, in Root, M.P.P. (Ed.) *Racially Mixed People in America.* Newbury Park. CA: Sage.

Harman, V. (forthcoming) *A Study of the Formal and Informal Support Networks of Lone White Mothers of Mixed-Parentage Children.* PhD Thesis, Royal Holloway, University of London.

Henriques, F. (1974) *Children of Caliban.* London: Secker and Warburg.

Holland, R. and Holland, K. (1984) Depressed Women: Outposts of Empire and Castles of Skin, in Richards, B. (Ed.) *Capitalism and Infancy on Psychoanalysis and Politics.* London: Free Association Books.

Ifekwunigwe, J. (1999*) Scattered Belongings: Cultural Paradoxes of 'Race', Nation and Gender.* London: Routledge.

Katz, I. (1996) *The Construction of Racial Identity in Children of Mixed Parentage: Mixed Metaphors.* London: Jessica Kingsley.

Maximé, J. (1987; 1991; 1994) *Black Identity: Workbook One; Black Pioneers: Workbook Two* and *Mixed Parentage: Workbook Three,* of the Black Like Me Series. EMANI Publications.

Maximé, J. (1987) Racial Identity and its Value to Black Children. *Social Work Today,* June 15.

Maximé J. (1993) The Importance of Racial Identity for the Psychological Well-being of Black Children. *Association for Child Psychology and Psychiatry Review and Newsletter,* 15: 4.

O'Donoghue, M. (2000) *White Mothers of Biracial, Black-White Adolescents: Negotiating the Borders of Racial Identity, Culture and Ethnicity.* PhD Thesis, New York University.

Okitikpi, T. (2001:2002) Communicating with Children of Interracial/Interethnic Parentage. *BSU/ IUC Journal of Social Work,* 4.

Prevatt-Goldstein, B. (1999) Black, with a White Parent, a Positive and Achievable Identity. *British Journal of Social Work,* 29: 285–301.

Ribbens, J. (1994) *Mothers and Their Children: A Feminist Sociology of Childrearing.* London: Sage.

Richards, W. (1995) Working with Mixed Race Young People. *Youth and Policy,* 49: 62–72.

Robinson, L. (1995) *Psychology for Social Workers: Black Perspectives.* London: Routledge.

Rosenblatt, P.C., Karis, T.A. and Powell, R.D. (1995) *Multiracial Couples: Black and White Voices.* Newbury Park, CA: Sage.

Tizard, B. and Phoenix, P. (1993) *Black, White or Mixed Race? Race and Racism in the Lives of Young People of Mixed-Parentage.* London: Routledge.

Twine, F. (1999) Transracial Mothering and Anti-racism: The Case of White Birth Mothers of 'Black' Children in Britain. *Feminist Studies.* Fall, 546–729.

Twine, F. (2003) Racial Literacy in Britain: Anti-racist Projects, Black Children, and White Parents. *Countours: A Journal of African Diaspora.* Fall, 1: 2.

Verbian, C. (2003) Counseling and Therapy with White Birth Mothers of Black/White Biracial Children: Addressing Racialised Discourses in Feminist and Multicultural Literature, www.oise.utoronto.ca/depts/aecdcp/cmpconf/papers/verbian.html

Wilson, A. (1987) *Mixed Race Children: A Study of Identity.* London: Allen and Unwin.

Chapter 9

Permanent Family Placement for Children of Dual Heritage: Issues Arising from a Longitudinal Study

June Thoburn

Introduction

Before describing and discussing the findings from a follow-up study of children of mixed race parentage placed with permanent substitute families in the early 1980s, it is important to put the research in context. Our understanding of the complex interaction between 'race', religion, culture, class, identity and biography has deepened since Jane Rowe and I designed the first study in 1984 (Fratter et al., 1991), and identified the sub-sample of children of minority ethnic origin for more detailed study in the mid 1990s. In particular we used the terms 'ethnic' and 'ethnicity' when we were referring to children and parents who were visibly different, perhaps more appropriately referred to as 'racialised' groups because they were likely to be treated differently and exposed to racism because of the colour of their skin (Prevatt-Goldstein, 2004). Physical appearance and the culture, religion and country of origin of the kinship group (a child's 'heritage') are clearly important components of identity but it is recognised that the geographical, social class and emotional environment in which a child grows up interact with heritage in contributing to an adult sense of self and self-esteem (see Rutter and Tienda, submitted, for a recent discussion of the 'multiple facets of ethnicity'). The 'nature-nurture' questions that have permeated the debates on 'race' and 'ethnicity' are, of course, central to the issues raised by a study of permanent placement with a substitute family.

In the report of the research, after much debate and consultation, we settled on the term 'mixed race parentage', since the focus was on children who were visibly different from the majority in UK society and had 'one white parent and one of minority ethnic origin' (Thoburn, Norford and Rashid, 2000: 8). It was evident in the 1980s, and is still evident from the voices of young people looked after away from their families (Timms and Thoburn, 2003), that skin colour and other physical characteristics, as well as aspects of heritage and culture of the birth family and the substitute family, are central to identity and self worth. The Children Act 1989 recognised this by requiring an authority proposing to look after a child to give due consideration to 'a child's religious persuasion, racial origin and cultural and linguistic background' (Children Act 1989, Section 22, 5, c).

Since the children were placed, children of mixed heritage, though still in a minority in the general population and only 3.2 per cent of all English children, form a much larger group than in the early 1980s and have more role models and peers who are of mixed heritage (Modood et al., 1997; Thoburn, Chand and Procter, 2004). Within this broad grouping, other major changes have taken place in the biographies of mixed heritage families in the UK. For example, Sinclair and Hai (2002: 16), using the broader definition of ethnic group to include white European children of different cultural, religious and linguistic backgrounds, reported that in Islington in 2002, '58 per cent (of the children looked after) are from minority ethnic groups, including refugee children. Within this group 34 per cent are from mixed heritage backgrounds'. Although the 2001 census and DH/DfES statistics have now replaced the single category of 'mixed' with four categories, the Sinclair and Hai study is a reminder that official statistics still fail to report the complexity.

The longitudinal study

The population was already, in the 1980s when we started our study, far more diverse than was recognised by the single category 'mixed race' that appeared in the official figures. Amongst our sample of children of minority ethnic origin were children whose parents were of five broad ethnic groups (including white European as a separate group), with the largest group of the parents (60 per cent) being of African-Caribbean heritage. However, there was considerably less diversity than now. In Neil's (2000) study of a cohort of 168 children placed for adoption in England in 1999 when aged under four, 32 (19 per cent) were of minority ethnic origin. Eleven of these had both parents of the same ethnic origin, but, in contrast to the 1980s cohort, in only one case were both parents of African-Caribbean origin whilst both parents of seven were of South Asian origin – a reversal of the position in the 1980s which mirrors the changes in the population as a whole. In contrast, a pattern more similar to that in the 1980s emerges when the 21 children who were of mixed heritage are considered. Fifteen (71 per cent) of those of mixed heritage had one parent of African-Caribbean origin, a similar proportion to the 73 per cent in the 1980 sample of children of mixed heritage, where this information was available. For 12 of these 15, the other parent was white; one had an Afghan parent and one had an African parent. There were two children of white/South Asian heritage (noticeably fewer than those with two South Asian parents) two of white/Burmese heritage and two of white/African heritage. However, the pattern is even more complex because, amongst the 42 parents of children of mixed heritage were 14 who were themselves of mixed or dual heritage.

When the different linguistic and cultural heritage of some of the white children is considered, the complexity of the present day task of placement workers in seeking to find families who can meet the needs of these children to understand and value their heritage becomes even more apparent. It is certainly no easier than it was twenty years ago.

There are other important differences between the children of mixed heritage being placed for permanence in the 1980s and now. When Rowe and Lambert (1973), wrote about children in unplanned long-term care, it was found that a disproportionate number of these 'children who wait' were black or Asian and many were in children's homes. Research and practitioners in the USA and then in the UK provided evidence that children who were past infancy could be successfully placed with new families. Of particular relevance to this chapter was the success of fostering and adoption teams in the UK in challenging the institutionally racist assumption that adopters would not want to adopt black children, which had led to them remaining in care when their parents had requested adoption. Initially this tended to be with white families (Raynor, 1970; Gill and Jackson, 1983). However, with the appointment of more black social workers and the pioneering work of adoption and fostering agencies and local authorities, black and Asian parents were recruited (Arnold and James, 1989; Rhodes, 1992).

In summary, the profile of the black and mixed heritage children placed with substitute families in the early 1980s differed from that of today in that many more were older and were living in children's homes. Also, a larger proportion than is currently the case had been in care for long periods and no longer had meaningful links with members of their birth families. The majority had, prior to their placements for adoption or permanent fostering, been placed with white foster or residential carers and often they lived in parts of the country where there were very few ethnic minority families. They were more likely to have been exposed to overt or inadvertent racism from individual carers and to institutionally racist policies and practices. Many of the research studies describing cohorts of minority ethnic children brought up in care date from this period, including our own. Ince's (1998), detailed account of the impact of being brought up in care during these years provides powerful testimony to the destructive impact it had on some children of dual heritage as do some of the adult adopted people quoted by Kirton, Feast and Howe (2000). Articles in the practice literature (for example Banks, 1992; Maxime, 1993) eloquently and movingly describe these young people and the strategies worked out to try to counteract the harm caused by inappropriate placement and individual and institutional racism.

Another difference concerns the issue of parental consent to placement. In Neil's study, ethnic minority children comprise almost 30 per cent of the 64 children who were placed at the request of their parents. However, those of mixed heritage were more likely than children both of whose parents were black or Asian to start to be looked after when past infancy. These differences are linked to the fact that the children with two parents of minority ethnic origin were younger at placement (mean age 12.6 months, compared with 16 months for the children of mixed heritage and 18.7 months for the white children). For the purposes of this chapter, the most interesting point is that parents of mixed heritage children found themselves in a situation where they had tried to care for their children before coming to the conclusion that they should request, or accede to the suggestion of social workers, that their children should be adopted. This sort of detail is not available for the 1980s cohort, which in any case involves a wider age range. However, there is a marked difference from the Neil study in that, in the 1980s, it was the children of mixed heritage who were more likely than those with two parents of minority ethnic origin to be 'voluntarily' relinquished as infants. The corollary is that, whilst those of mixed heritage in the 1980s sample were *less* likely to be in touch with birth parents immediately before and after placement than was the case for those with two ethnic minority parents, the opposite was the case for those placed more recently.

The characteristics of 171 children of mixed heritage placed for adoption or permanent foster care in the early 1980s

The study built on an earlier survey and analysis of rates of disruption (between three and eight years after placement), of a total cohort of 1165 placements of children with adoptive or permanent foster families not previously known to them, made by 24 British voluntary adoption agencies between 1980 and 1984. There were 246 placements of children of minority ethnic origin (Fratter et al., 1991). That study found that children born to two parents of minority ethnic origin were no more likely than white children to experience disruption, when age at placement and other mediating variables were held constant. However, children of mixed heritage were more likely to experience placement breakdown. It was also noted that, at that time, placement practice for children of mixed race parentage was more like that for white children than for children with two black or Asian parents, in that white and mixed heritage children were less likely than black or Asian children to retain contact with a birth parent and to be placed with a sibling.

For the follow-up study focusing specifically on children of minority ethnic heritage, a purposive interview sample was identified including broadly equal numbers of families where children were placed trans-racially (which we defined as with two white parents) and with families where at least one parent was of minority ethnic origin. Since there were few 'same race' placements in the original sample, we contacted a local authority known to be successfully recruiting minority ethnic families as adopters or long term foster parents in the early eighties. When these cases were added, 297 children were included in the background sample, in respect of which files were scrutinised and information on the children, their birth parents, their new parents and social work practice was analysed. Outcome was measured in terms of whether the placement was known to be intact or to have broken down at the time the file was scrutinised (Charles, Rashid and Thoburn, 1992; Moffatt and Thoburn, 2001). For the 51 young people in the intensive interview sample, qualitative data including information on a wider range of outcome measures, were analysed thematically. Standardised schedules were used in order to measure self-esteem and well-being. Particular emphasis was placed on the satisfaction of the young people and their adoptive or foster families with the placement service and the parenting or growing up experience, and to the issues of racism, ethnic identity and adoptive identity.

Of the children in the background cohort, 172 (56 per cent) were of mixed heritage. Due to the lack of precision in the records as to the ethnic background of parents who were described as 'mixed race' or 'mixed ethnicity' it is not possible to know how many placements were of children of dual heritage and how many of a more complex mixture of heritage and culture. Almost half (around 80 out of 172), had a dual African-Caribbean and white UK heritage; around 20 (12 per cent), were of South Asian and white British descent and 12 (7 per cent) were of black African and white British descent. The children ranged in age at the time of placement between a few weeks and 15 years, with the mean age being six. The children of mixed heritage tended to be younger than those with two ethnic minority parents, a factor that we had to bear in mind when looking at any differences between the two groups. Almost half of the children of mixed race parentage were under four at placement (44 per cent) compared with only a quarter of those with two parents of the same minority ethnic background. At the other end of the age range, almost half of those with both birth parents of minority ethnic origins were aged nine or over. This age difference in part explains why 65 per cent of the children of mixed heritage but only 41 per cent of those with two black or Asian parents were placed for adoption rather than as permanent foster children (x^2: 19.547; df: 2; p<.0001). Also related to age is the finding that more of the children with two black or Asian parents (47 per cent), were recorded as needing to have some post-placement contact with a birth parent, compared with 20 per cent of the children of mixed heritage (x^2: 14.162; df: 3; p<.01).

There is too little data on the attitudes of the birth fathers to placement plans. Where available for the mothers (in just over half of the cases), 57 per cent of the mothers of children of mixed heritage, compared to 37 per cent of the mothers of children both of whose parents were of minority ethnicity, were recorded as agreeing with the plan. Nevertheless, the birth mother opposed the placement of almost a third of the mixed heritage children. 27 per cent of the children of mixed heritage compared with 43 per cent of children with two minority ethnic parents were placed with a sibling (x^2: 8.129; df: 1; p<.01).

Only 23 of the mixed heritage children (13 per cent – mainly infants) had no 'special needs' or 'obstacles to placement' and a further 18 (10 per cent) had only one. Over half had emotional or behavioural difficulties at the time of placement; half had a history of abuse or deprivation; 57 per cent had experienced three or more moves in care and 28 per cent had already had one disrupted 'permanent' placement. A marked difference from the situation today is that around 40 per cent joined their new families from a children's home or hospital and only 58 per cent from foster care.

Returning to other background factors, the records were less than adequate as to the heritage of ethnic minority parents born overseas, and were rarely more specific than 'Asian' 'Pakistani' or 'Caribbean'. For the cohort as a whole, the religion of the birth mother was recorded in only two thirds of cases and the religion of the birth father in less than half of the cases. This paucity of information was commented on by some of the ethnic minority adopters who, in order to talk with the child about their heritage, wanted to know in which community or on which Caribbean island the child's parents were brought up. One of the reasons why they welcomed contact with the birth parents was so that they could fill in the gaps.

In the light of our present more complex understanding of culture and heritage which includes social class and differences between urban and rural cultures, it is important to note that, from what we could glean from the often inadequate data on the files about the circumstances of the birth parents, most, but not all, of the birth parents were on low incomes. Gender is another important aspect of identity. Of the 101 children with a white parent, this was the father in 20 cases and the mother in 81 cases. There were five mothers and three fathers of mixed race parentage.

The new families

Turning to the new families, a large majority of these children of mixed heritage were placed with white parents (84 per cent compared with 55 per cent of those both of whose parents came from a similar ethnic background – x^2: 32.76: df: 2; p<.0001). Only sixteen (11 per cent) were placed in a mixed partnership family with one white parent (as were 14 [12 per cent] of children both of whose parents were of minority ethnic origin). Eight (5 per cent) compared with a third of those with two ethnic minority parents were placed in families in which both parents, or the single parent, were black or Asian. It was even less likely that they would be placed in a family of the same faith group as one or both of their birth parents. Only 13 were placed with new parents of the same ethnic and religious group as at least one of their parents; one was placed in a Muslim family of a different ethnic background and five were placed in a family of the same ethnic group but with a different religious and cultural background.

In other important respects the culture in the new families differed from that of their birth families. The new parents were more likely to be in higher income groups and were more likely to live in rural or suburban areas. In this respect also their experience differed from that of children with two minority ethnic parents who were more likely to be placed with Caribbean or South Asian parents living in working class or more socially and ethnically mixed neighbourhoods. Whilst it was more likely that in their families of origin the mother was white and the father was of minority ethnicity, in the new families, the balance was more even with 15 of the new fathers and 19 of the new mothers being of minority ethnic origin. 19 of the new parents were of African-Caribbean ethnicity, only three were of South Asian origin, three were of mixed heritage and one was of black Africa origin.

Looking at the characteristics other than ethnicity, it was more likely that the under fives would be placed with a white or a mixed partnership family and that those aged nine or over would be placed in a family where both parents (or the single parent) were African-Caribbean or Asian. Six of the eight children placed with two parents of minority ethnicity were aged nine or over.

There were significant differences in terms of whether the children had continuing birth family contact after placement. This is an important variable since one way for children placed in white families to stay in touch with and learn more about their heritage is to have continuing links with the birth family. This is especially so if they are in touch with their ethnic minority parents but even if only linking with the white side of the family they are able to ask questions about the other half of their heritage and have a better chance of seeking out their father and extended family as young adults. Only 18 per cent of the mixed heritage children had any face-to-face contact with a birth parent after placement and 9 per cent of those who did not see a birth parent had some contact with a sibling placed elsewhere or a relative. This is in contrast to the 38 per cent of children with two minority ethnic parents having contact with birth parents (x^2: 14.326; df: 1; p<.0001). This is explained partly by the fact that the mixed heritage children were younger and fewer of their birth parents sought contact, but mainly by the fact that the new families where both parents were of minority ethnic origin were more likely to think that continuing contact would be in the children's interests and to facilitate it (Rashid, 2000). Coupled with the fact that children with two minority ethnic parents were more likely to be actually living with a sibling, it can be seen that, in terms of continuing links with the heritage and culture of their first family, they fared considerably better than those of mixed heritage.

Outcomes for the children

The only outcome measure we have on the background cohort of 297 children is whether or not the placement was known to be ongoing or to have disrupted between ten and 15 years after placement (though in some cases information had petered out at an earlier stage). The age range at this time was between 10 and 30, with around three quarters being over the age of 16. At the end of the survey period, according to the recorded information, 67 per cent were still with their adoptive or foster families and a further 12 per cent were living independently or had formed their own families but were still in close contact with the adoptive or foster family. Information was missing in respect of some of the young people, but three were known to have returned to live with birth parents, four were living independently following disruption of the placement and for 29 the placement had disrupted and the young person was in care, custody or their whereabouts not known.

When age at placement and other variables such as the child's behaviour at the time of placement was taken into account, there was no difference in rates of disruption between children of mixed ethnicity and those with two parents of minority ethnic origin. This more positive finding from that in the original survey is probably explained by the slightly different composition of the two groups, with the addition of infants to a sample, from which they were originally excluded.

Once other variables were controlled for, there was also no difference in breakdown rates, either for the children with two parents of the same minority ethnic background or for those of mixed heritage, in terms of whether they were placed in white, mixed partnership or black or Asian families.

What the young people and their foster or adoptive parents had to say

Because we were aware of the limitations of this narrow definition of 'success', it was to the adoptive and foster parents and the young people themselves that we turned for information on a wider range of outcome measures and a greater understanding of their experiences of adoptive/foster family life. One or both parents was interviewed in respect of the 34 families of 51 of the young people (there were sibling groups of two and three) as were 24 of the young people themselves. The African-Caribbean and Asian members of the research team conducted most of the interviews. The research interviews were all in the homes of the parents or of those young people who had set up their own households, and sometimes their partners joined in. For those who were old enough to remember, they were usually lengthy and involved going back over the period of coming into care and through the placement experience to the present situation. In addition to these discussions, standardised schedules on self-esteem and physical and mental health were completed and questions were specifically asked to allow for a 'researcher-rating' on the young person's sense of pride in their ethnic identity and heritage and comfort with being adopted or fostered.

This was a purposive sample selected to include children of mixed heritage and those with two minority ethnic parents, and also to include broadly equal numbers placed with white families and placed with at least one parent of minority ethnic origin. Twenty-four of the 51 young people were of dual or mixed heritage, thirteen of them having been placed with at least one parent of minority ethnic origin and 11 placed with white parents. Fourteen had been placed for adoption and seven as permanent foster children (though one had been adopted by his foster parents at the age of 17). Six had had some direct contact with a birth parent during the placement and two had contact with a sibling placed elsewhere or another relative but not a parent. Four grew up with at least one birth sibling but 17 were placed alone. The interview sample was broadly representative of the main sample in that 79 per cent of all the placements were 'successful' in that the young person was still living in the family or living independently but with strong links. However, more of the mixed heritage children in the interview sample were in the 'successful' group in that 19 were either still living in the family home (ten), or had set up their own households but were in close touch (nine). One was living with a birth parent and one was in residential care following a disruption. We were only able to interview two young adults whose placements had ended unhappily for themselves and their adoptive families, but heard from parents in cases, where the placement had disrupted, of the deep distress of all family members and their continuing anxiety for the future well-being of the young people. However, as with the quantitative findings, the findings from the interviews were generally positive. The majority of the young people in the interview sample were coping with life reasonably well and were feeling at ease with themselves as people of mixed heritage, although some, especially the young men, spoke of times when they were reminded that they were seen by both parts of their heritage as 'different'.

> *With me being both, it depends who I'm with. I can be really posh with my white friends, but with my black friends I'd just be black. Because my dad was black and my mum was white, I'm not hundred per cent black or hundred per cent white. Some of the clubs I go to I get taken the Mickey out of me. I've been called 'greyhound'.*

It is important to look for some explanation of why the outcomes for these young people (including those placed with white families), were more positive in nearly all respects than those reported by some other researchers. To a large extent, the answer lies in the way this and other samples were identified. It is not possible to have a fully representative sample when 'volunteers' are invited to tell their stories, but the way in which they are contacted in the first place makes a difference. Most of those interviewed for other studies had contacted a post adoption service for assistance, whereas this applied to none in our sample of families contacted randomly from a full list of placements. In order to locate our conclusions, based on what the young people and their parents had to tell us, the reader needs to have a more detailed picture of our interviewees. Of the ten young people of mixed heritage interviewed (for whom more detailed measures of well-being were available than for the 14 in respect of whom we only had the views of the parents), six were under four at the time of placement and therefore had the scales weighted towards success, but three were over nine when placed. Nine of the ten had been adopted. Seven were of African-Caribbean and white British heritage; two were of South Asian/white and one of African/white heritage. Six were placed with white families, two were with families that matched their birth heritage and one young man of African descent grew up with a mother of African-Caribbean heritage and a white British father. None of the placements of these ten had disrupted although in some cases the adoptive or foster parents had separated. Only one had continuing face-to-face contact with a birth parent throughout the placement though some had, as young adults, reconnected with birth parents or siblings with whom they had lost touch. Eight were rated as successful taking on board all the outcome measures, two in some respects and none entirely unsuccessful, although one 15 year old (who already had many problems by the time he was placed at the age of three with a white adoptive mother and African-Caribbean father), told the researchers that there were times when he was unhappy with his adoptive family and wanted to leave. Three were under 18 at the time of interview and seven were young adults (including four over 22 and well able to use the benefit of hindsight). All those aged over 18 were in work or higher education.

It is not possible in a short article to do justice to what the parents and children had to tell us. The richness of what they had to say is reported in detail in the full report (Thoburn et al., 2000) and in Rashid's (2000) article focusing on the strengths of black families. Of most relevance to this volume is what the parents and young people had to say about their attitudes towards 'race', racism, heritage and culture and about growing up with a family of a different heritage and appearance from their own, or in a family of a similar ethnic or cultural background. The first point of difference between these families in which a child of mixed heritage was living and those where parents and children were all of minority ethnicity is that, whether placed with white parents, mixed partnerships or two black or Asian parents, these were all 'mixed heritage' families. Family ties in all but a small minority of cases became strong, and all the parents interviewed empathised with the issues around visible difference and racism that impacted on their partners or children, and tried to find ways of helping them overcome obstacles and fight battles. Perhaps because of this, they had given more thought to the meaning of heritage than had some of the black and Asian families for whom the issues appeared more straightforward. The white parents in mixed race partnerships were particularly sensitive to the impact of racist behaviour on their partners and on their children but felt less able than their black or Asian partners to find appropriate ways to help the children:

> *I know like all people in mixed marriages that I as a white man am treated in the same bank, in the same shop, in the same everywhere in a way which is different to the way my wife is treated. The same bank and the same money, and my wife would have to give her address, and she is terribly affected by this. Some places they don't see her for years because they have the cheek to ask for some form of identification.*

> (Thoburn et al., 2000: 118)

Unlike those interviewed by Gill and Jackson (1983) (and indicating how social work practice at the recruitment and approval stage had moved on even by the 1980s) none of the families thought that racism, discrimination and heritage were irrelevant to their family life. We concluded that the ethnicity, faith group, and other aspects of the culture of the new family had an important bearing on *how* the parents set about the task of integrating an, often vulnerable, child into their family. This was particularly the case with respect to ways of helping the growing child to develop strategies for overcoming the effects of racism and to develop a positive sense of their heritage. But all the parents interviewed placed some importance on these tasks and on their role of ensuring that, as young adults, all avenues would be open to their sons and daughters, so that they were able to choose whether and when to live within one culture rather than another. This twenty-year-old of African-Caribbean and white heritage paid tribute to her white adoptive mother:

> I am very conscious and very interested in black culture. I am still learning today. My mum knows that. I'm more into my blackness than my white side- a lot of that is down to my mum.... And I respect her for that. I don't find it a problem. I find being black a positive thing. I think I feel more black than white at the moment because of the friends I have got now and the area I am living in now.
>
> (Thoburn et al., 2000: 141)

The task was particularly difficult for both white and black parents when a child had been socialised, before joining them, into thinking of itself as white and had developed racist stereotypes. A white foster mother of brothers placed in their early teens when their children's home closed down said:

> I think it is very important for them to feel proud of their ethnic identity, but how you do that is a different matter, especially if they have grown up thinking they are white. I think it's hard for a white person to do that. I think they were damaged in terms of their own self-image and culture. So we just did our best with what had already been done. It's a pragmatic thing. I think in a perfect world they would have been placed in families that reflected their racial and cultural heritage.

Several of the black parents interviewed talked about 'shadism'. This foster mother was shocked by the attitudes and language of an eleven-year-old placed with her from a children's home in a rural area:

> He was very damaged. He had lost his identity. He would talk about 'Bournville Selection'. I said 'Hold on a minute. You are either black or you are white, and you are black.' 'I'm not', he said, 'I'm a light darkie'. I got really worried because I didn't realise that there were black children who had got sold down the line like that.
>
> (Thoburn et al., 2000: 126)

The ethnicity of the adoptive or foster parents also had a bearing on the strategies of the young people. Those in white families tended to address issues around 'race', identity and biography later than was the case for those living with at least one parent of minority ethnic origin. The most common message from the young people was that they loved their parents dearly, and would not want to change anything about them, but most of those brought up in white families recognised that there had been times when their parents had not been able to understand some of their thoughts and experiences around their different appearance and heritage. This was especially so when they lived in parts of the country where there were few peers and role models who were of mixed heritage:

I wouldn't change anything about my family. But at the end of the day I wouldn't advise any black person to go to a white family, because you miss out on all the culture and everything. But I do appreciate what they did for me. There is nothing I would change about what they did for me.

(Thoburn et al., 2000: 143)

Taking into account our quantitative and qualitative findings we concluded that some white families can successfully meet the needs of children of mixed heritage, especially if they live in ethnically mixed communities. But white families have extra obstacles to overcome, which can make a challenging form of parenting (parenting of a child by adoption or fostering) even more challenging. Our overall conclusion was that:

The requirements of the Children Act 1989 to seek to place children with parents who can meet their identified needs as individuals, and who are of similar cultural and ethnic background, provide a sound basis for policy. This would be the view of all but a tiny minority of the parents and children who gave their opinions on this question, including members of ethnically mixed and ethnically similar families.

(Thoburn et al., 2000: 206)

Conclusion

Readers of this chapter will differ in their conclusions as to whether a study of children placed in the 1980s is still relevant to those seeking to place children today, when so much about our society and practice has changed. It is an 'endemic' problem for child placement research, since it is not possible to know whether a placement has been a success or otherwise until the child placed, perhaps as a baby, is a young adult, by which time practice has moved on. In terms of the survey results, some changes have occurred that will have worked towards reducing the likelihood of disruption. Most workers now have a much better understanding of the impact of individual and institutional racism and of the complexity of ethnicity and heritage. This is in no small part due to the recruitment to family placement teams and post-adoption services of more social workers of minority ethnic heritage, including some who were themselves brought up in care or with adoptive families and some who were themselves adopters or foster parents. Children placed for adoption now are on average younger; more of them are removed at birth and placed before they have been seriously maltreated. On the other hand, they are as likely now, as then, to have been exposed to several moves in care and those placed when older are more likely to have experienced very serious neglect as a result of the addictions of their parents or witnessing domestic violence. They may gain from the fact that they are less likely to have lost all contact with their parents, but this can make them more vulnerable unless pre-existing relationships with family members and previous carers are understood and respected.

Turning to the changes in adopters and long-term foster carers, with a very few exceptions, the new families in the study reported here were entirely unknown to the child they were matched with. More placements now are pre-existing foster placements confirmed as adoptive or permanent foster placements, and the success rate for these is higher than for 'stranger' placements. Especially for those of white British and African-Caribbean heritage, the 'pool' of families of the same heritage from which adoptive and foster families can be recruited is much bigger. The biggest differences, however, are demographic and societal, resulting in most children of mixed heritage who come into care having far more peers and role models of similar culture and physical appearance to themselves than was the case for the young people described in this study.

In pointing out these differences, it is not my intention to underplay the harm still suffered by ethnic minority children by inappropriate policy and practice, nor to downplay the relevance of studies of children placed in adoptive and foster families in the 1980s. The impact made by these earlier research studies in giving voice to the young people and their carers, and by social workers and therapists who have sought to find ways of repairing some of the harm (for example Banks, 1992; Maxime, 1993), contributed to the emphasis placed in the Children Act 1989 on the importance of heritage, religion and culture. In Neil's (2000) study, none of the children both of whose parents were from one of the major ethnic communities in the UK population was placed with two (or a single) white parent and in most cases there was a close match in terms of religion and culture. This was also the case for eleven of the children of mixed heritage. However, three were placed with parents of a different minority ethnic origin and six children, all with three white grandparents, were placed with white families. Neil's findings on the broad success of adoption workers in respecting the heritage of most of the young children they place finds only partial corroboration in the data in the National Adoption Register's first report (2003). Only five per cent of the children on the register were of Asian or black heritage and there was a broad match, in terms of ethnicity, with those wanting to adopt (four per cent were of Asian or black heritage). The difficulty here, as with the white children and prospective adopters, lies in the mismatch between the sorts of children the adopters are hoping to have placed with them (mostly children under three with few problems) and the characteristics of the children waiting for adoptive families. However, this contrasts with the mismatch between the 510 children of mixed heritage (17 per cent of the children on the register) and the 190 mixed heritage families seeking to adopt.

A book specifically devoted to children and families of mixed heritage is timely. It provides an opportunity to highlight that it is far more difficult to find new families who are of the same ethnic, religious and cultural origin for a significant minority of the children of mixed heritage needing substitute family placement in the 21st century. They are the ones who will either wait longer in care before being adopted by families of similar heritage; remain in unplanned and often unstable care; or be placed with families whose appearance and culture differ significantly from those of their birth families. Sadly, it is this group of children who are least likely to have continuing contact with their families of origin which can go a long way, if the contact is arranged so that meaningful links are maintained, to counteract some of the difficulties inherent in trans-racial placements. This is in part because adoption agencies have still not recognised the desirability, and, I would argue from research, the feasibility of maintaining birth family links for most young children placed for adoption (Neil, 2000). The lack of continuing links with the first family is also because this group of parents is least likely to ask to maintain even indirect contact. In some cases this is because any knowledge of a relationship with a white man, evidenced by the birth of a child may place the mother in danger; and sometimes because of their high mobility, including returning to their country of birth.

For these reasons studies of children of mixed heritage growing up, in the main, with white families, may still have something to tell us about how practice can help the mixed heritage adoptive kinship groups of the future. These studies also have relevance for the children adopted from overseas who are, in the broad sense of the term, growing up in mixed heritage families. Many of them will choose white partners and some of their children will need permanent substitute family placement in the future. There is evidence to support this hypothesis from mainly Scandinavian research on inter-country trans-racial adoption (Lindblad et al., 2003) and from the accounts of adults adopted trans-racially and across national boundaries (Armstrong and Slaytor, 2002).

Finally, some social workers now will be working in adult mental health or child and family teams with parents of mixed heritage who suffered from being placed with substitute families who failed to understand the importance of heritage and added to the harm they had already suffered. In reporting that in this study the majority of these placements worked well, or well enough, a caveat is essential that around one in five of them resulted in disruption; and some of those whose placement did not break down wished that someone had picked up on their unhappiness and placed them somewhere else. These children and adults are under-represented in this study but their voices are heard in the work of the other researchers cited in the introduction. We know from the statistics that many parents of children in care were themselves in care or adopted. They carry the double burden of unhappy experiences of care and their failure to keep their own children out of care. From the over-representation in care over the last decade of mixed heritage children, it is safe to assume that increasing numbers of parents of looked after children will be of mixed heritage.

But there are important positive messages in our study. The majority of these children, despite the extent of their problems, did well enough and some did very well indeed, going on to higher education and careers in the professions and the arts. In terms of the research agenda, the need now is to move on from the debate about 'same race' or 'trans-racial' placements. The emphasis should be placed on looking at how mixed heritage adoptive or foster kinship networks (including birth families) can be helped to ensure that the proportion of successful placements is even higher, and that the lessons from both successful and failed placements are learned and built into training and practice.

References

Armstrong, S. and Slaytor, P. (2001) *The Colour of Difference: Journeys in Transracial Adoption.* Sydney: The Federation Press.

Arnold, E. and James, M. (1989) Finding Black Families for Black Children in Care: A Case Study. *New Community,* 15: 3, 417–25.

Banks, N. (1992) Techniques for Direct Identity Work with Black Children. *Adoption and Fostering,* 16: 3, 19–25.

Charles, M., Rashid, S.P. and Thoburn, J. (1992) The Placement of Black Children with Permanent New Families. *Adoption and Fostering,* 16: 3, 13–9.

Fratter, J., Rowe, J., Sapsford, D. and Thoburn, J. (1991) *Permanent Family Placement: A Decade of Experience.* London: BAAF.

Gill, O. and Jackson, B. (1983) *Adoption and Race: Black, Asian and Mixed Race Children in White Families.* London: BAAF.

Ince, L. (1998), *Making it Alone: A Study of the Care Experiences of Young Black People.* London: BAAF.

Kirton, D., Feast, J. and Howe, D. (2000) Searching, Reunion and Transracial Adoption. *Adoption and Fostering,* 24: 3, 6–18.

Lindblad, F., Hjern, A. and Vinnerljung, B. (2003) Intercountry Adopted Children as Young Adults: A Swedish Cohort Study. *American Journal of Orthopsychiatry,* 72: 2, 190–202.

Maxime, J. (1993) The Importance of Racial Identity for the Psychological Well-being of Black Children. *Association of Child Psychology and Psychiatry Review,* 15: 4, 172–9.

Modood, T., Berthoud, R., Lakey, J., Nazroo, J., Smith, P., Virdee, S. and Bershon, S. (1997) *Fourth National Survey of Ethnic Minorities in Britain: Diversity and Disadvantage.* London: PSI.

Moffatt, P.G. and Thoburn, J. (2001) Outcomes of Permanent Family Placement for Children of Minority Ethnic Origin. *Child and Family Social Work,* 6: 13–21.

Prevatt-Goldstein, B. (2004) Introductory Chapter: A Context for the Review, in Thoburn. J., Chand, A. and Procter, J. (2004) *Child Welfare Services for Minority Ethnic Families: The Research Reviewed.* London: Jessica Kingsley.

Raynor, L. (1970*) Adoption of Non-white Children: The Experience of a British Adoption Project.* London, Allen and Unwin.

Rashid, S.P. (2000) The Strengths of Black Families. *Adoption and Fostering,* 24: 1, 15–22.

Rhodes, P.J. (1992) *'Racial Matching' in Fostering.* Aldershot: Avebury.

Rowe, J. and Lambert, L. (1973) *Children Who Wait.* London: ABAFA.

Rutter, M. and Tienda, M. (submitted). The Multiple Facets of Ethnicity, in Rutter, M. and Tienda, M. (Eds.) *Ethnicity and Causal Mechanisms.* New York: Cambridge University Press.

Sinclair, R. and Hai, N. (2003) *Children of Mixed Heritage in Need in Islington.* London: NCB.

Thoburn, J., Norford, L. and Rashid, S.P. (2000) *Permanent Family Placement for Children of Minority Ethnic Origin.* London: Jessica Kingsley.

Thoburn. J., Chand, A. and Procter, J. (2004) *Child Welfare Services for Minority Ethnic Families: The Research Reviewed.* London: Jessica Kingsley.

Timms, J. and Thoburn, J. (2003) *Your Shout!* London: NSPCC.

Chapter 10

Mixed Race Children: Policy and Practice Considerations

Gillian Olumide

Introduction: The Nature of Race and Race Thinking

It is customary, when speaking or writing of race and mixed race, to begin with a disclaimer along the lines that race is not 'real'. It has no biological foundation, it is a social construct, and nobody in their right minds would ever admit to acting on the basis of race thinking. We might also be confronted with the view that, although race is not 'real', it is an essential aspect of individual psychology or identity, or that, although race is not 'real', it is nevertheless an important concept in forms of political mobilisation (the list goes on). In fact, the choice is not a straightforward one between biology and social construction. This distinction between the 'real' world of biology and the 'unreal' worlds of the social and political is problematic. It seems that race is, if not 'real', then thoroughly reified through discourses which employ race thinking. It is a well understood construct which often forms a basis for action in daily life.

How is it possible, in this (sur)real world of race thinking, to speak meaningfully about a matter which does not really exist, and yet which has such enormous influence on thinking and action? How are we to discuss perceived differences between people? How is it possible to account for differences in social experiences and unequal access to social goods and services which flow from such ranked percep-tions of difference? More to the point, since this is an enquiry into *mixed* race, what are the social mechanisms that prevent falsification of the evidence on race and deny social space to those wishing to experiment with alternatives to race thinking – a nourishing activity sometimes enjoyed by those defined in relation to mixed race?

It is sometimes said that race is socially constructed. Katz (1996), in a discussion of identity formation in mixed race children, takes this view and calls upon Berger and Luckmann (1966), for an explanation of the social construction of reality. He goes on to explain the ordering of society through institutional regulation, and the playing out of individual roles within the constructed reality, in order for individuals to participate in the social world. He arrives at the view that:

> The relationship between institutions and roles, therefore, is that when people act in accordance with the rules of institutions, they are acting in roles.
>
> (Katz, 1996: 30)

There are questions of particular importance here for the mixed race child – and for everyone else too. If one is assigned a 'role' and is bound, in some way, to act this out, is it then essential to have a '*role model*' of similar appearance to ones self who is bound to act in a similar 'role' and does this with particular zest? Or are we free to look around at people we may admire on the basis of any feature we wish (honesty, scientific achievement, cheerfulness, excellence at sport, weighing over 20 stone, for example) and emulate these selected features? For those perceived as mixed, there is a particular difficulty over 'roles' since 'institutions' seem to be unremittingly confused over what a 'mixed role' might be. If such 'roles' are socially constructed, it follows that they can be un-constructed or deconstructed and reconstructed if we accept that there is, in addition to structure, the *agency* (however constricted) of individuals and groups to effect this change. We may need a little more information as to the how or why of social ascription, since humankind has a predilection for action outside its proper 'roles' and hence its capacity for movement and transformation and revolution.

Birkitt (1991) tackles the question from a different angle, in a consideration of limitations to the ways in which we are able to influence the development of our 'social selves' (or to exercise agency). In this argument, it is ideologies arising from particular forms of social, political and economic organisation which create social divisions and hinder the range of personality development. As he writes: 'Social inequalities and unnecessary controls on behaviour, which keep ruling groups in power, still divide us' (Birkitt, 1991: 241).

It is the acknowledgement of the centrality of ideology, and the recognition that social divisions serve a purpose beyond that of individuation, that gives depth to Birkitt's argument. Also, there is the acknowledgement that from ideologies of race all manner of power, interests, privileges, denigrations and blessings flow and are held in place. Whilst we may be aware of a limited range of socially ascribed positions available to us (on the basis of gender, race, ability, age and so on) it is usual for individuals and social groups to dispute these positions and strive to negotiate more favourable options. The 'baby boomer' generation's dispute with the notion of 'growing old gracefully' can be used to illustrate this. We are, at the very least, entitled to enquire into who is benefiting from the maintenance of these positions, and how best things might be altered in an individual or group's own favour. This may be what social work is currently attempting to do for mixed race children 'in care', an enterprise to which this book makes an important contribution.

As to the provenance of race ideology, there are various positions. There seems to be some agreement, within social science at least, that there is no linear development of the concept and that it is differentially applied with very different outcomes. Of great value here is work which seeks to unearth the different episodes of race thinking and to find links and patterns in the career of race thinking. These works include Hannaford, 1996; Fryer, 1989; Goldberg, 1993; Bauman; 1973 and 1989, and many others which contribute to our thinking on the subject.

Before moving on to a consideration of public policy, it will be useful to suggest an understanding of the nature of race – a working definition from which to proceed. Race is a false category, and hence the understanding that it is not 'real' but ideological (Gilroy, 1987, discusses ideological work in connection with race). Much has, however, been built on the back of this mystification of the human condition. It is an ideology through which claims to provide explanations of selectively perceived human differences are made; such differences are often ranked and ordered. They also form the basis for counter claims by groups who recognise a similarity of interests and wish to mobilise around such ideological principles in order to overcome or better their collective position. Racism may be seen as the operationalisation of race thinking – that is to say argument or action that proceeds from the premise that race has explanatory value in human affairs. Anti-racism, in this understanding, is opposition to action or argument based on race thinking.

This is perhaps a departure from convention in this area. It does, however, serve to problematise 'race' rather than incorporating it into anti-racist discourse. It also enables *mixed* race to be challenged as an ideological construct instead of the rather unsatisfactory rag-bag of bits and pieces of identity, appearance and split cultural affiliation which is its status at present. The tasks for the (perceived) mixed race constituency also change from being attempts to meld together components of a 'multiple heritage' (which seems to be a 'role') to those of quizzing the very idea that such a thing is possible or necessary. It requires a shifting of the responsibility, long shouldered by populations defined as mixed, from the group itself to the perpetrators of race thinking.

Public Policy and Welfare Agents

Turning now to the question of mixed race in public policy, it is an interesting exercise to debate the historical similarities between welfare organisations such as the Liverpool Association for the Welfare of Half Caste Children, the Hanoi Society for the Protection of Metis Youth and the Aboriginal Protection Boards in Australia. Each was, through public policy and political will, founded to protect the perceived welfare interests of mixed race children and, in each case, this involved a paternalistic endeavour which often involved separation of mixed race children from their families 'for their own good'. This is not to suggest an international conspiracy to disrupt the lives of those considered to be mixed race. It does, however, suggest a certain recurring vulnerability amongst mixed race families in contexts of race thinking. An outstanding similarity between these and other attempts to cater for the welfare of the mixed race is that definitions of 'welfare' never included the views of the defined. (For further discussion of these welfare agencies and their underlying aims, please see, for example, van Krieken, 1999; Stoler, 1995; Olumide, 2002). Another point to bear in mind is that, with the benefit of hindsight, it may be suggested that in the processes of defining the 'needs' of mixed race children *mistakes have been made.*

Just as there is no case for an international conspiracy theory in relation to mixed race (although plenty of evidence of the portability of discourses such as those around 'race' and Eugenics), it would be simplistic to suggest a direct link between historical disruptions and the present UK situation in which disproportionate numbers of children defined as mixed enter the public care system. In a much-quoted study by Bebbington and Miles (1989) the authors undertook a quantitative investigation of the notes of children looked after in a local authority. They placed 'mixed race', along with poverty, poor housing and other markers of social disadvantage, as a risk factor in shaping the likelihood of a child's reception into care. They further suggest that even where other factors remain constant, mixed race children are two and a half times more likely to enter care than any other group. It is certainly an urgent necessity to enquire further into the nature of this risk. What are the factors that produce and reproduce the riskiness of a mixed race definition?

This is a question which is beginning to be examined, Okitikpi, 1999b; Barn, 1999; Banks, 1995. Barn looked for common factors in the backgrounds of the children in question. According to Barn the majority profile of mixed race children looked after is of a single white mother over the age of 26, and absent Afro-Caribbean father, both of whom are likely to be unemployed or, in the cases where father's employment details were recorded, employed in semi-skilled or unskilled manual work. Barn also enquires into the situations of these mothers and raises concerns about wider issues, which may have some bearing on the breakdown of the families in question. Social and family support, isolation, racism, inadequate education and identity issues are put forward as possibly affecting the experiences of mixed race families.

It is also possible that welfare agents dealing with such families carry their own responses to this family type. Okitikpi (1999b) and Banks (1995) both consider this possibility and each suggests that the failure of some social workers to 'think outside the box' of current racial definitions leads to a pre-determination of the circumstances of the mixed-racialised child as being intrinsically problematic. Further, that because of these processes of racialisation, questions of 'entitlement' arise – and where but in the (sur)real arena of race thinking could a mother's 'right' to her child be the subject of serious debate? My own work in this area (Olumide, 1997) led me to examine the professionalisation project of social work. It appears expert knowledge about 'race' has formed part of the claims to exclusive knowledge which are an essential aspect of professionalisation processes. A question to note here is whether there are now movements towards claiming expert knowledge in the area of *mixed* race.

There is no plan here to revisit the *cause celebre* of the 1980s and 90s, Social Services 'same race' policies in fostering and adoption (which were argued in slightly different forms in the US and UK). These arguments are well catered for in work such as Hayes, 1993; Macey, 1995; Allen, 1994 and Olumide, 1997. Sufficient to say that these policies betrayed the extent of race thinking in policy and practice and were yet another *mistake* in the growing catalogue of mistakes in relation to mixed racialised children and their similarly designated families. A short quotation from the British Association for Adoption and Fostering (BAAF) can be used to illustrate the nature, if not the magnitude, of this mistake. This is from one of BAAF's Social Work Practice Notes, Number 13, which was first issued in 1987 and reissued in 1995. This quotation deals with 'some questions we are frequently asked':

1a   Are children of mixed parentage really black?

Children of mixed parentage who have a white and a black parent are no different to other black children. Almost invariably they will be identified as black by society…Such children, with parents from different races (sic), should feel good about having one white and one black parent. Society will make them feel good about being white. It follows that the children are best placed in homes which will redress this balance and make them feel good about being black too.

There is no Such Thing as Society

Of course, there *is* such a thing as society (otherwise there would be no sociologists, and then where would we be?). However, the society of this particular practice note does appear to be a realistic construction of events. Nor is its logic born out in any meaningful way in the lives of most of society's members. There does not, at this point, appear to be great merit in summoning labyrinthine arguments to unpick this piece of confused thinking and nor do we need to examine closely the lives of white people whom society 'sees' as white yet has manifestly failed to make feel good about themselves, in order to refute the advice (social work case loads are full of such examples).

There is more of this 'seeing' society to be discovered if we move to the question of what to name mixed racialised children. Calls, such as that by Prevatt-Goldstein (1999), for the social legitimisation of racialised titles such as 'black-with-a-white-parent' (a modification of even-if-they-look-white-they-are-really-black school of thought) or, as Okitikpi (1999a) argues, an essentialist argument based on the 'one drop rule' for children considered to be of mixed race, does nothing much to address the question of race thinking. The premise that 'society sees these children as black' is unsophisticated, it requires qualification. So also do other terminologies of mixed race from the older 'half caste', 'mixed blood' and 'mulatto' names to the more modern 'mixed parentage', 'mixed heritage', 'multiple heritage', 'multiracial' and 'mixed race'. We need to know much more about this process of perceived mixture and cannot allow such terminology to pass without comment. Mixed *racialised*, on the other hand, has a more realistic and embracing quality and permits the defined to place the burden of race thinking at the feet of the race thinker. It conveys succinctly a social location within the 'seeing' society and, moreover, it suggests an awareness of social processes of racialisation that convey such distinctive social experiences. It is a knowing term, which frees the user from the tasks of describing the nature of their perceived mixture and from acceptance of an ambiguous social location. It deserves consideration.

The Cart: Elements of Mixed Racialisation

I shall, at this interim point, discuss some tentative conclusions about what I have come to call the production of the 'mixed race condition' (by which I mean commonality of experience amongst the many populations, past and present, socially defined in relation to race mixture). This may appear to be a case of putting the cart before the horse. There is method in this arrangement, however, as I will then move on to discuss evidence of mixed race experience with a loose framework in place for organising this authoritative body of experience. This may well be a contribution to practical thinking about mixed racialised experience and may also contribute to debate within the welfare professions on the subject of how to comprehend the experiences of looked after children. My conclusions are the result of an examination of historical, written and sociological evidence about the social construction of mixed race.

Primarily, mixed racialisation involves the construction of mixed race as an *ambiguous social location*. It is not usually embraced unconditionally by any of the racially defined groups who regard themselves as homogeneous, although mixed populations have been used instrumentally in various causes – yet are just as likely to be rejected and reviled. To compound the constructed ambiguity, social definition may shift rapidly. In one decade, for example, they are (in the case of looked after mixed racialised children) 'really' black, in the next they must 'own' their individual and multiple 'heritages'. They are neither fish nor foul, and must expend considerable resources on the discovery of a comfortable social retreat, which may shift over the course of a lifetime.

Mixed race as a social location is also a *contested site,* because it is constructed in terms of ambiguity it is readily available to be reconstructed and drawn into various arguments and purposes. There are many historical examples of such contest over the loyalty of mixed groups (Olumide, 2002) and the phenomenon can be clearly illustrated with recourse to the kinds of street abuse frequently reported within the mixed race constituency. This often involves allegations of disloyalty to some 'unmixed', and alternatively racialised group. The mixed person or partner is said to display an insufficiency of racial characteristics, has less of a grasp of the 'culture' of the group than is desirable, has made poor choices of partner or parents, is generally a 'race traitor' and therefore is quite unable to fit in. If, on the other hand, loyalty to a particular group is courted, the mixed racialised person or family is flatteringly admitted to the group for as long as they remain silent about their reservations about the limitations of a 'pure' designation and suppress information about their full range of cultural affiliations.

Another feature of mixed racialisation is that it is constructed in terms of inadequacy and inability to conduct its own affairs. (Although research such as that of Tizzard and Phoenix, 1993, shows otherwise). There is a notion that *dependency* is a feature of the 'mixed race condition' and this can be dependency on more unitary racialised groups for acceptance or on the benevolence of social agencies to organise for particular 'needs' amongst the mixed racialised. Linked to all these is *conditionality,* a strong feature of mixed racialised life. It is inevitable that racialised groups practise conditionality as a means of securing the loyalty and the attention of those they define as mixed – to do otherwise would be to slither on what Zack (1993), calls the 'slippery slope of mixed race' with the danger that this might reveal that homogeneity is rather more mixed than it is comfortable to imagine. Conditionality has a great price, and this is often measured in the information a mixed racialised person or family must suppress about them selves in order to become acceptable.

A final point I wish to make about the mixed racialisation project is that it often becomes a *point of articulation* in projects beyond racialisation. It is very apparent that ideologies of class contribute to the production of inequalities of social and economic outcome. It is no coincidence that it is an archetypal 'single white mother' that causes considerable attention in the discussion of a mixed racialised problem-to-be-solved in relation to looked after mixed racialised children. To trace the patterned connections in these social events it is necessary to go beyond a conceptualisation of social 'roles' to the fabric of social construction. Those constructed as poor and female are immensely disadvantaged when faced with the conditionality inherent in the social construction of whiteness. Mixed racialisation confers abnormal social disadvantage on all women (Frankenberg, 1993; Olumide, 2002). In relation to the public care system, this seems currently to affect disproportionately (although this has not been universally so) white women with mixed racialised children. That association with race mixing has been such a British social taboo (for women, and not just white women) and is now somewhat (possibly temporarily) relaxed, may account for the increased numbers of mixed racialised children in care. There are simply more children with this designation and more women with the racialised social experience that renders them so perplexingly vulnerable.

In the next section I will discuss the interplay of this loose structure and *agency* by drawing on information from those required to grapple with a mixed racialised ascription.

The Horse: The Quality of Mixed Race Experience

The real drivers in this (or any) enquiry into mixed racialisation are the analyses available within the group. Not only is this the definitive source of information about the effects of mixed racialisation, those within the group also offer complex theoretical perspectives on social processes that create their experiences: Root, 1996; Tizzard and Phoenix, 1993, and many others demonstrate this. As a part of my doctoral research (Olumide, 1997), I interviewed 35 people in mixed race situations in different parts of the UK, and collected data from two workshops about mixed race families at conferences for women who were active in their communities in Bradford, West Yorkshire. There was a good deal of interest in the subject and many informal conversations and unsolicited letters and telephone calls also contributed to the store of data. It was clear that whilst all were very much aware of the limitations imposed by their social positions, such positions were not beyond dispute and certainly not beyond analysis. I approached people for the varieties of their associations with mixed race – as a social ascription, mixed race touches where it falls and there are some remarkable similarities of experience between different sub groups of people sharing in the mixed race condition.

The research population includes an age range from teens to seventies, and different permutations of mixed race – including people with knowledge of constructions of mixed race in other parts of the world. Most of the people in the study had not been adopted or fostered, although several engaged with the debate over transracial adoption and felt that it enabled public commentary on mixed race more generally. Two people had adopted their children and one of two people who had been put into care at birth had gone on to foster and to adopt her own family. During interviews and in the workshops, I simply asked people to talk about their experiences that they felt stemmed from their association with mixed race. In analysing these data, my aim was to present them in as transparent a manner as possible; the experiences are grouped into five main themes. **Gains** contain the positive assessments of mixed race – of which there were many. **Issues** collected a range of mixed race issues which were described as having confronted either the speaker or people within their social world. The theme **Social Analysis** groups some of the attempts to theorise or to account for aspects of mixed race experience. It is on the twin themes of **Sanctions** and **Strategies** that I will concentrate here. This material contains information and insights into some of the pressures and negative social experiences of those identified with mixed race as well as the responses devised to protect and rebut such negativity. A single study can only claim to be a snapshot, but nevertheless it is a snapshot of the priorities nominated within the mixed racialised population.

Sanctions

Perhaps the most debilitating of the reported sanctions was the **rejection** by family of relationships and children perceived to be of mixed race. Reports ranged from complete rejection to less absolute, but highly uncomfortable, rejecting behaviours. I interviewed two people who had been placed in the public care system from birth (during the 1960s). In one case, a sister of the white birth mother had been poised to adopt until it transpired that the baby – my informant – was 'coloured' and the family adoption plans were cancelled. In the other case, the mother had not been in a strong, independent position herself, and her own mother had withheld any support until adoption of the baby was agreed. There are accounts of struggles to hold onto children and partners in the face of severe opposition and isolation from families. It was also recognised that where a relationship was in difficulty there was often little support available for discussion or for leaving the relationship.

There was little doubt that families are in a prime position to disrupt relationships they perceive as mixed and this sanction was applied to all kinds of mixed racialised situations including a white woman whose five children were from three different fathers, including an African man. The woman was aware that her mother discriminated between the children to the extent that in buying presents the 'darkest' child received the least attractive and valuable gifts. In order to protect her children from this inequity, she had much reduced contact with the mother.

The **looks of strangers** was an experience mentioned by everyone I spoke to. 'Looks' was a well understood means of registering perceived difference, and conveying disapproval. A woman of white English/Cypriot parents with four children by an Afro Caribbean man said:

> *I think it's mostly the stares. But I mean I still get that now. And I think I've learned not to look, not to feel the stares, whereas other people with me still feel them.*

A young mixed race woman (white UK and black Caribbean born parents) considering experiences with different boyfriends, said of her current relationship:

> *With a white guy I seemed to get a different atmosphere. With a black guy there's not really that problem. People look at you and it seems to feel right. You don't get the same stares that you did as a mixed couple.*

Her boyfriend (British with black Caribbean born parents) confirmed this, indicating that his partner was acceptable if they were perceived as a black couple:

> *We've had no reaction really. It's much easier than with white. If you're with a black girl it seems that's right…It's like they're saying 'stick with your own kind.'*

People could also identify parts of towns, places and neighbourhood where they could move free from 'looks'. There were specific places to avoid if possible. Even where no exchanges took place beyond looks, these looks alone were disturbing and seemed sufficient to exert a controlling influence.

A more active form of controlling behaviour reported by most and understood by all the people in the study was **abuse**. This might be in verbal, written or physical form, and there were differences in severity and frequency of experience, with racialised name calling amongst school children and abusive comments from complete strangers in the street being very widely reported. The content of verbal abuse shows that those considered to be mixed or mixing race are a highly differentiated population, and of particular importance seems to be gender difference. Some of the racialised content was wildly inaccurate, but most was highly gender specific.

Examples of this were a pregnant white British woman married to a British man with Pakistan born parents having a car driven at her by erstwhile (white male) school colleagues shouting 'get that Paki baby out of you'. Also a young Nigerian born man, walking with a young Anglo-Indian woman reported similarly aggressive behaviour. The woman was evidently perceived as white and the young man was chased, verbally and physically threatened. This raises all sorts of questions about the differential experiences of those who are considered to 'look mixed race' and those who do not.

Reputation was a particularly important sanction for the women in the study and, although there were discernible differences between lighter and darker skinned women, attack on reputation is a very fundamental aspect of mixed race (and mixed religious) experience. An almost routine experience reported amongst white women concerns the differences in response between going out alone and with family members. One woman, speaking during a workshop gives a flavour of a very well understood experience:

> *As a white woman out on my own, I can go anywhere. As a white woman with my black kids I am called names. As a white woman out with my kids and a black man, I am a 'white bitch' and my kids are 'black bastards'.*

A light skinned Caribbean born woman with a relatively darker daughter told of her experiences with gossiping neighbours when she gave birth to a much lighter second child. The neighbours had ostracised her, believing that her (also Caribbean) husband could not be the father of the second child:

> *Mother: 'One day I invited them (the neighbours) round for coffee. I said, 'I know what you're going round saying'. They didn't know where to put their faces. I said, 'I'm not angry, but I thought you'd like to know it's not true'. They didn't understand. I'm not really very black, neither is my husband. So usually the children have a lighter skin. They started thinking, well it has to be a white man. Well I'm used to this from the West Indies. It's acceptable, because if you're of mixed race....'*
>
> *Daughter: 'Anything can happen'.*

The confidence to take on this sort of situation is not always available to individuals. Also, the onus for rectifying these sorts of assumption is a heavy additional weight to carry for many people.

Several women told their (mainly white in this sample) mothers' stories of experiences of giving birth to children perceived as mixed race:

> *When she gave birth to one of my sisters the midwife left the room because as the head appeared with an obviously big mop of hair, the midwife said to her, 'you're married to a foreigner', and left the room. The funny thing was, and the way my mum tells it, in a jokey way, because she wasn't actually married at the time, which would have been much worse.*

For the black women in the study, the attack on reputation came mainly from two directions: the first on their motives for entering a relationship perceived as mixed and the second on notions of betrayal. A Ghanaian born woman, in the company of her white, English husband reported being shouted at in the street by several black men and addressed as 'Hey, sister'. The substance of their communication was to the effect that she might be better suited by a black partner, since by being seen with a white man she was 'betraying' herself, the black male population and black people more generally. She had the presence of mind to stop and enquire, 'and is this how you treat your sister?' This notion of 'betrayal' of the group was also reported as an attack on the reputations of some of the black men, either in casual street abuse or in more intimate conversations with friends, where choice of partners was challenged.

The privileges, often spoken of as belonging to people of an undifferentiated white population (although, as I have already suggested, privilege has never been very evenly distributed) are evidently withdrawn in the face of perceived race mixing. Two white women discussed this point with me as follows:

Sue: They think that black and Asian men don't have no right to go out with white women, and you know if you've been with a black man, you're a slag. They do...

Jo: Nigger lover...and with that kind of attitude, yes, they think you're a slag, and that's all you get. When you've got kids you can't lie about it. I've got used to it now. You shouldn't have to lie about it anyway.

Jill: Do you think the reputation sticks?

Jo: Yes, it gets around

This matter of who is 'entitled' to associate with whom is of interest to the mixed race constituency. I suggested above that mixed race is a contested site and such notions of who is entitled to mix with who is a part of this. So too, in the context of 'looked after' children, is the question of who is best placed to look after the mixed race child.

Pigeonholing was considered a very serious sanction amongst the people I spoke to. It refers to the tendency to place individuals within pre-determined racial or ethnic groupings, or to transform mixed race into something more definite. Its seriousness, for those considered to be mixed or mixing race, is linked to questions of difficulties over the naming of mixed race and to other routine denials of social space and rights, such as the right to self-define.

The pigeonholing experience was generally regarded as a curtailment of choice over self-identification and a comment on how and with whom one may reasonably live. People also expressed it as a pressure on relationships between partners and their children where each were perceived as being so fundamentally 'different' from the others as to undermine their validity as a unit. In particular, pressures to 'choose' between bi-polar racially defined groups was often seen as an unwelcome and embarrassing restriction, and often formed the basis of strong individual critiques of racial ordering during interviews. The conditionality attached to having to 'choose' was often perceived as unnecessary and artificial.

Repatriation is a common strand of racialised experience, and also a feature of racial abuse as in the routine 'go back home' and 'go back to where you belong' comments. The quest to repatriate does not, however, always come as gratuitous street abuse, it may occur during the course of social conversations. This is problematic to partners and their children perceived as being of completely different origins. (Even where they may have grown up in the same neighbourhood and attended the same schools). The question of 'home' and belonging is particularly acute for those perceived as mixed or mixing race. Whilst it is evident that enquiries in the area of repatriation are aimed at locating individuals 'elsewhere', there are frequently multiple potential 'elsewheres' within a family history or, conversely there may be no alternative 'home' to declare, making this category of experience particularly complex for kith and kin within the mixed race group.

A final sanction concerns constructions of the **unsuitability** of mixed race families – they are, on the basis of the data, often not perceived as belonging together and nor are people perceived to be mixed race expected to be entirely comfortable with their situation but rather to be searching for 'who they really are'. There are reports, amongst the respondents, of pre-marital advice about not having children because of the difficulties they might face. One couple were asked, during their wedding interview with their minister, whether their reason for getting married was the male partner's desire for British citizenship.

White women, in particular, also found that their parenting skills were sometimes in question (see also Okitikpi, 1999b). Several had been accused of racism and failing to nurture healthy 'racial identities' in their children. One single white mother, whose son had a particularly piercing voice, was suspected by a neighbour of harming her children because of the son's noise, audible from the small flat. She became so concerned that the neighbour would involve an agency such as the NSPCC that she attempted to involve the health visitor as an ally in pre-empting any allegations. Many white women had been made aware of the notion that their children were, in some essential but non-specific way, very different from themselves. Most seriously, many mothers felt undermined by the situation and, where isolation from others in a similar position was an issue, felt alone and sometimes quite overwhelmed by the situation.

This is a very brief review of a large body of negative social experiences reported by the people to whom I spoke. It would, however, be quite wrong to suggest that these sanctions were passively met.

Strategies

One of the universal strategies for dealing with these and other mixed race experiences was to seek out others with sympathetic views and comparable experiences. Sometimes this was for ease of friendships with people with similar social experiences. For others the seeking was in order to explore aspects of experience that had been suppressed. People sought out others defined in similar ways to themselves, some had even moved home to be able to live in 'mixed' areas. This seeking out behaviour appears to be the beginnings of an acknowledgement of common purpose amongst those defined in association with race mixing. There is a new determination, now well underway, to make visible and to theorise the experiences of *mixed racism*.

Another strategy adopted by some people was to challenge negative perceptions of mixed race. For some this was expressed as a duty to themselves or their families. Others felt that their very existence was sufficient challenge to ideas about race and racial separatism. Parents had gone to great lengths to engage with schools over their children's experiences of racism and one parent had been prepared to provide literature portraying mixed race families and people in a positive light. In the area of a lack of positive portrayals of mixed race (this may have altered quite recently with mixed race being adopted as a 'trendy' advertising motif, although not one without a 'hidden agenda' ripe for deconstruction as to its implied ambiguity and instrumentalist intent) several parents spoke about ways of overcoming the deficit of positive images often using photographs of their own children.

Most parents of young children were acutely aware of the need to deal with mixed racism and many felt that it was their responsibility to equip their children with positive versions of their family make up and instant rebuttals of negative comment and behaviour. Others felt that extra effort would be required in order for children to achieve their potential in life and that educational achievement would be a necessary means to success. Some people used humour to laugh off foolish prejudice and negativity. There was a widespread awareness of the value of adjusting behaviour and language to adapt to broad cultural ranges, what Maria Root (1996) describes as practicing 'situational ethnicity'. The ability to move between cultural ranges was highly prized by many in the study and was cited as beneficial in work and private lives.

More complicated strategies included the construction of 'imaginary homelands' which encompassed 'lost' or suppressed aspects of cultural background as well as the contacting of absent parents as part of a general gathering together of all parts of individual history into a comfortable sense of ownership and one-ness. For different reasons, often involving the conditional aspects of mixed racialisation, many people in the study had been forced to conceal aspects of their history or to postpone a full appraisal, sometimes well into adult life – this was so of mixed race people but also for partners who had needed to suppress their own histories in order to be acceptable within a partner's family or social group. Once able to struggle free they had experimented with different ways of reconciling their personal stories (sometimes 'borrowing' from cultures they found interesting) into a satisfying order. A dramatic example of this activity was a man in his 60s of Scottish and Nigerian parents. He had been raised in Nigeria and told that he was the son of his mother's brother. During his early life with his uncle and aunt he was aware that information was being concealed and eventually learned the truth about his birth parents. He stowed away on a Liverpool bound ship and made a life in England. In his 50s he decided to seek out his birth mother in Nigeria and was reconciled just prior to her death. These episodes of construction (often reconstruction) were expressed as being of immense importance in people's lives bringing relief and personal acceptance.

Implications for Policy and Practice

Having run through some aspects of experience it is time to draw out some possible uses for such insights. Public policy, as I have already hinted at, has historically tended to take a heavy hand to the putative problems of race mixing. It has tended, along with a great deal of the research literature on mixed race, to locate such problems *within* the group itself with the implication that outcomes such as family breakdown and parental inadequacy are an outcome of race mixing *per se* rather than responses to it. There is, with the slow turning of the social services discourse concerning mixed race children (Barn, 1999; Boushel, 1996; Okitikpi, 1999a and 1999b), an opportunity to include mixed racialisation as a factor in understanding the production of social exclusion.

A main aim for both policy and practice is to include the views of the target group – the mixed racialised. There is currently a fashionable rhetoric around user-practitioner partnership, which has yet to be fully realised in relation to the mixed race constituency. Nowhere is it more important to lay aside prejudices and to discard folk law definitions of race than in the care of vulnerable mixed race children and their families and to *listen* to their realities and beliefs and wishes. This, as Okitikpi and others have suggested, means that practitioners must study their own reservations and beliefs about mixed race to ensure that pessimistic and partisan views are not acted upon.

Within public institutions, an attention to analyses of race which are capable of producing a version of anti-racist philosophy that *does not* depend on race thinking and the acceptance of bipolar racialised groupings, would assist policy and practice. This is the province of social work education and training, which has, in recent history, produced some very debatable versions of anti-racist practice.

There is also an urgent need to investigate more fully both the extent and the underlying reasons for the disproportionate numbers of mixed race children in the public care system. This is a mistake that has persisted for far too long without remedy nor understanding.

Professionalisation processes and the claiming of 'expert knowledge' in areas of life, which once people managed for themselves is fraught with problems. There is no 'ought' about a matter such as adopting a particular 'racial' identity or holding a particular view about cultural diversity. Those claiming expertise in such matters, which are rightly in the private domain, will inevitably impose their collective will at the expense of individual freedom. Pigeonholing is, certainly amongst my research sample, one of the severest curtailments of mixed race freedom.

Racialisation of the mixed race group is particularly perplexing as it constructs mixed race people and families as inherently pathological, confused and fragile. Moreover, this is reinforced by all manner of research into these presumed deficiencies. Such assumptions simply cannot go unchallenged or continue to be acted upon. There are certainly, as I hope I have been able to begin to show here, pressures on those racialised as mixed. Depending on social circumstances such pressures can be very burdensome and may well benefit from intelligent and well-directed social support. However, with the wisdom of history and hindsight, it seems particularly necessary to attempt to avoid past mistakes, which have proved so detrimental to mixed race groups. To proceed in partnership with the clientele is above all to become aware of the quality of mixed racialised experience. I have offered a tiny range of examples of the pressures and responses which form part of such experience. Much, much more information and analysis is needed.

References

Allen, S. (1994) *Sociological Perspectives on Adoption: The Policy Implications of the Transracial Discourse* (Unpublished paper). University of Bradford.

BAAF (1995) Practice Note 13.

Banks, N. (1995) Children of Black Mixed Parentage and Their Placement Needs. *Fostering and Adoption,* 19: 2.

Barn, R. (1999) White Mothers, Mixed Parentage Children and Child Welfare. *British Journal of Social Work,* 29: 2.

Bauman, Z. (1973) *Culture as Praxis.* London: Routledge and Kegan Paul.

Bauman, Z. (1989) *Modernity and the Holocaust.* Cambridge: Polity.

Bebbington, A. and Miles, J. (1989) The Backgrounds of Children Who Enter Local Authority Care. *British Journal of Social Work,* 19: 5.

Berger, P. and Luckmann, T. (1966) *The Social Construction of Reality.* New York: Doubleday.

Birkitt, B. (1991) *Social Selves: Theories of the Social Formation of Personality.* London: Sage.

Boushel, M. (1996) Vulnerable Multiracial Families and Early Years Services. *Children and Society,* 10: 4.

Frankenberg, R. (1993) *White Women, Race Matters: The Social Construction of Whiteness.* London: Routledge.

Fryer, P. (1989) *Black People in the British Empire: An Introduction.* London: Pluto Press.

Gilroy, P. (1987) *There ain't No Black in the Union Jack: The Cultural Politics of Race and Nation.* London: Hutchison Education.

Goldberg, D.T. (1993) *Racist Culture.* Oxford: Blackwell.

Goldstein, B.P. (1999) Black with a White Parent, A Positive and Achievable Identity. *British Journal of Social Work,* 29: 2.

Hannaford, I. (1996) *Race: The History of an Idea in the West.* Baltimore: John Hopkins University Press.

Hayes, P. (1993) Transracial Adoption: Politics and Ideology. *Child Welfare,* LXX 11: 3.

Katz, I. (1996) *The Construction of Racial Identity in Children of Mixed Parentage: Mixed Metaphors.* London: Jessica Kingsley.

Macey, M. (1995) Same Race Adoption Policy: Anti-Racism or Racism? *Journal of Social Policy,* 24: 4.

Okitikpi, T. (1999a) Identification of Mixed Race Children. *Issues in Social Work Education,* 19: 1, 93–106.

Okitikpi, T. (1999b) Mixed Race Children in Care: Why so Many? in *Child Care in Practice, Northern Ireland Journal of Multi-Disciplinary Child Care Practice,* 5: 4 October.

Olumide, J. (1997) *The Social Construction of Mixed Race: An Enquiry into the Experiences of Those so Designated and into the Agency of Professional Cultures in the Production of Racialised Social Ascriptions.* PhD Thesis. University of Bradford.

Olumide, J. (2002) *Raiding the Gene Pool: The Social Construction of Mixed Race.* London: Pluto Press.

Prevatt-Goldstein, B. (1999) Direct Work with Black Children with One White Parent, in Barn, N. (Ed.) *Working with Black Children and Adolescents in Need.* London, BAAF.

Root, M. (Ed.) (1996) *The Multiracial Experience: Racial Borders as the New Frontier.* London: Sage.

Smedley, A. (1993) *Race in North America: Origin and Evolution of a World View.* Boulder: Westview Press.

Stoler, A. (1995) Mixed Bloods and the Cultural Politics of European Identity in Colonial Southeast Asia, in Pieterse, J.N. and Parekh, B. (Eds.) *The Decolonisation of the Imagination: Culture, Knowledge and Power.* London: Zed Books.

Tizzard, B. and Phoenix, A. (1993) *Black, White or Mixed Race? Race and Racism in the Lives of Young People of Mixed Parentage.* London: Routledge.

Van Kreiken, R. (1999) The Stolen Generations and Cultural Genocide: The Forced Removal of Australian Indigenous Children from Their Families and its Implications for the Sociology of Childhood. *Childhood,* 6: 3.

Zack, N. (1993) *Race and Mixed Race.* Philadelphia: Temple Press.